The Children of
Willesden Lane

The Children of Willesden Lane

BEYOND THE KINDERTRANSPORT: A MEMOIR OF MUSIC, LOVE, AND SURVIVAL

MONA GOLABEK AND LEE COHEN

WARNER BOOKS

An AOL Time Warner Company

Warner Books, Inc., 1271 Avenue of the Americas, New York, NY 10020

Visit our Web site at www.twbookmark.com.

An AOL Time Warner Company

Printed in the United States of America

First Printing: April 2002

10 9 8 7 6 5 4 3 2 1

ISBN: 0-446-52781-5

Library of Congress Control Number: 2002100990

Book design by Giorgetta Bell McRee

To my beloved mother, Lisa
The music of your soul is eternal

Acknowledgments

I would like to express my heartfelt gratitude to the many individuals who participated in the fifteen-year journey to bring my mother's story to life.

For her extraordinary insight and prose, enormous thanks are owed to Christine Burrill, without whom this book would not have been possible.

A profound thank you to Irene Webb and John Karas, for bringing the project to Warner Books; to Jamie Raab, for believing in the power of my mother's life story; to Caryn Karmatz Rudy for being our guiding light; and to Harvey-Jane Kowal and Molly Chehak for their invaluable support.

Thanks to Lee Cohen for his great caring and devotion to the project, and to those individuals who gave him support, guidance, and wisdom—Lois Sarkisian, Alex Cohen, Brien Lopez, Susan Grode, Regina Seidman Miller, Belinda Casas-Wells, Deborah Oppenheimer, Al Landolph and Pam Somers, Tara Cook, Mark and Ann Goldblatt, Fred and Cheryl Cook. In memory of Sue Cohen.

Thanks to Dennis and Gina Schwartz, Martin Lewis, Hans Cohen, Bertha Leverton, David Jedwab, Honey Chester, Annette Saville, for their time, generosity, and memories.

Thanks also to Richard Burkhart, for his daily commitment every step of the way; Chuck Hurewitz, for his invaluable advice; Marc Whitmore, for his thoughtful assistance; and to Jesse Silver, Jackie Maduff, and my brother-in-law, Marc Kaye, for their insightful contributions and loving support through the long process.

And finally:

The deepest thanks

To my best friend, my sister, Renée: We had the greatest parents.

To Michele: You were Lisa's angel.

To Sarah: Lisa loved you with all her heart.

To Jonathan and Rachel: Lisa is listening—and waiting to see where the music will lead you.

Author's Note

Several years ago, I was preparing for a concert that featured the Grieg piano concerto and found my thoughts turning to my beloved mother, Lisa. I remembered the last time I had played for her.

Although she had fought against it with everything she had, my mother had grown weak and fragile from illness. She yearned to sit at the grand piano in her living room and play, but she could no longer manage it. Instead, she watched and listened as I played.

As I began, I was a child again, her student, watching her at the piano, hearing her play those same heroic passages of the Grieg with a passion and intensity I knew would be difficult to match. My mother had lived an incredible journey and she had infused her music with everything she had experienced: her childhood with loving parents in Vienna before World War II; her escape to England aboard the legendary Kindertransport; her struggle to study her music while a war raged around her; and always, her endless fascination with that ramshackle building at 243 Willesden Lane, the hostel in the London suburbs where she lived as a young refugee separated from her family.

I watched my mother's eyes as I played for her, and remembered how I loved my piano lessons. They were more than piano lessons—they were lessons in life. They were filled with stories of the hostel and the people she knew there. Her stories were my folklore, filled with bits and pieces about a kind lady named Mrs. Cohen, a mysterious suitor named Aaron who whistled the melody of the Grieg as a signal to meet him, and members of a clandestine committee named Gina, Gunter, and Paul. Sitting at the piano, I would close my eyes and listen to her gentle voice, and see the world and the people she had grown up with and loved.

Most of the names you read on these pages are the real names of Lisa Jura's friends and family. Aaron's name has been changed, because this character was an amalgamation of several boys who were influential in my mother's life. Mr. Hardesty's character, too, represents several Bloomsbury House officials. The facts and conversations that follow reflect my mother's recollections, although I realize that some of her stories were clouded by time. In the places where there were gaps in her memory, my present-day research has filled them in. The spirit of the story is all hers.

When I finished playing for my mother that final time, she nodded her quiet approval and I moved to her bedside and sat there as she had sat at mine when I was a child. At the end, she was, I believe, at peace.

My mother was my greatest teacher, and my sister, Renée, and I became concert pianists because of her.

I know that Lisa Jura Golabek's spirit continues to live, not only through me, but through all those she touched. Her legacy has inspired my music and my life and continues to do so every single day. I pass along her story in hopes it may enrich the passion and music that lie in each of us.

The Children of
Willesden Lane

1

*L*ISA JURA took her appearance very seriously. She stood in front of the mirror for an eternity, arranging her dark red hair so that it peeked stylishly from under the wool hat she had just bought in the hand-me-down store. The hat needed the perfect tilt . . . just so. She had seen the models do it in the fashion magazines.

She was determined to look more sophisticated than her fourteen years. She was going to her piano lesson and there was nothing more important. Finally turning from the mirror, she smiled at the image of a saucy young girl.

After opening the front door quietly, so as not to disturb her family, she walked down the hallway of the crowded tenement and emerged from the solemn gray building, stepping onto the sidewalk of Franzensbrückestrasse in the heart of the Jewish section of the city.

As she had done every Sunday since her tenth birthday, Lisa boarded the lumbering streetcar and crossed Vienna, heading for Professor Isseles's studio.

She loved the ride.

The images rushed by her window—the glorious Ferris wheel of the Prater amusement park and the blue and serene Danube—eerily accompanied by the distant rhythm of an oompah band. To go across the city was to enter another century—the era of grand palaces and stately ballrooms. Street upon street of marble and granite, of pillar and pediment. The spire of St. Stephen's Cathedral danced by. Her father called it *"Der Alte Steffe"*—"Old Stevie." Lisa thought it a silly name; it was much more grand than that, rising to the heavens like a castle in a fairy tale.

As the streetcar descended the broad avenue and passed Symphony Hall, Lisa closed her eyes, just as she had many times before, and imagined herself sitting perfectly still in front of the grand piano on the stage of the great auditorium. A hush fell over the audience. The keys shimmered in front of her, ebony against ivory. She could hear the opening of Grieg's heroic piano concerto: the soft roll of the tympani building until the moment of her entrance. She straightened her back into the elegant posture her mother had taught her, and when the tension was almost unbearable she took a breath and began to play.

She could sense the excitement of the audience and feel their hearts beat in time with hers. The exhilaration of hearing the music inside her was so extreme that the bumps of the ride and the noise of the street no longer disturbed her.

When she finally opened her eyes, the car was passing the Ringstrasse, the majestic tree-lined boulevard where the Grand Court Opera House stood. She looked out the window in awe and waited for the driver to call her stop.

This was the Vienna of Mozart, Beethoven, Schubert, Mahler, and Strauss, the greatest composers of all time.

Lisa's mother had filled her head with their stories, and she had made a secret vow to live up to their legacy. She could hear their music in the marble of the buildings and the stones of the streets. They were here. They were listening.

In a booming voice, the driver called out her stop. But today his words were strange and different. In place of the familiar "Mahler-Strasse" she was expecting, he called another name: "Meistersinger-Strasse." Lisa's heart stopped momentarily.

She climbed down into the great plaza. All the street signs had been changed; the Nazis did not approve of such a grand avenue being named after a Jew. She felt her fury grow but tried to contain herself. Getting upset would only interfere with her music. She forced herself to think about the lesson ahead, knowing that once she was at the piano, the world outside would disappear.

Although it was early, the café-lined streets bustled with energy. The gentle sounds of the "Blue Danube" waltz, mixing with raucous Dixieland jazz, returned the smile to Lisa's face. The aroma of warm, fresh *apfelstrudel*, thick with sliced apples and cinnamon, made her long for a taste of her mother's recipe—surely the best in all of Vienna.

Inside the cafés, well-dressed young men and women sipped their coffee, deep in animated conversation. Lisa imagined them all to be composers, artists, and poets passionately defending their latest works. She yearned to join them, to wear fine clothes and speak of Beethoven and Mozart—to be a part of that intoxicating café society. One day, when she made her musical debut, these streets, these cafés, would be hers.

When Lisa reached her destination, she stopped short. A German soldier, tall and emotionless, stood in the doorway of the old stone building that housed Professor Isseles's music studio. The sun glinted harshly off the black rifle he held against his gray uniform.

She had been coming to the professor's studio for nearly four years, but this was the first time anyone had been standing guard. She shouldn't have been surprised, though; Nazi guards were becoming an increasingly menacing sight on the streets of Vienna.

He asked coldly, "What business do you have here?"

"I have a piano lesson," she replied, trying not to be frightened by the soldier's commanding presence or by the firearm on his shoulder.

"The professor will be waiting," she continued in a loud, clear voice, the force of her words belying her true state of mind. The soldier looked up to the second-floor window. A figure stared down, then motioned that it was all right for the girl to come up. Lowering his weapon, the soldier moved away from the door and grudgingly allowed Lisa to pass.

"Come in, Miss Jura," Professor Isseles said, greeting Lisa with his customary warm handshake. The stoop-shouldered, white-haired gentleman ushered her in past a chipped bust of Beethoven and a sideboard covered with stacks of yellow sheet music. She breathed in the aroma of the professor's pipe tobacco. These sights and scents had become a friendly greeting—a signal that for the next hour, she could turn away from all else and be a part of the music she loved.

The professor's stately Blüthner piano stood in the middle of the studio. It was richly polished, with ornately carved legs and a scroll-patterned music stand. On the wall hung her teacher's prized possession—a photograph of Franz Liszt as an old man, surrounded by several students, including the professor's teacher. He boasted that his teachings were a direct line from the master himself, and there was a worn mark on the photograph where he had so often placed his finger.

As usual, there was little small talk. Lisa put the score of Beethoven's Piano Concerto no. 1 in C on the music stand and sat on the worn piano bench. She adjusted its height to fit her small stature.

"So, Miss Jura, was it difficult?" asked the professor.

"It was much too easy," she teased.

"Then I expect nothing less than perfection," he responded, smiling.

Lisa began to play the tender C-major opening theme. The professor sat forward in his chair and followed her progress with his copy of the score. When the simple theme erupted into cascades of descending arpeggios, she peered out of the corner of her eye to judge his reaction.

She hoped to catch him smiling. After all, she had learned the complicated first movement in only a week and had often heard him say that she was his best student.

But the professor continued listening with a stern concentration. When he had this expression, she imagined it was his sadness at not being able to play the piano anymore. Arthritis had stiffened his fingers, making it impossible to demonstrate the correct way of playing. What a cruel trick of fate to deny a pianist the ability to perform, she thought. She could not imagine a day when she would not be able to play.

To illustrate his lessons, Professor Isseles would play recordings for her on his gramophone. He was in awe of Horowitz's playing of Rachmaninoff, but it was the lyri-

5

cism of Myra Hess performing Beethoven that he most appreciated.

"Listen to the tone of her legato," the professor would say with a sigh.

Lisa listened and listened and listened.

For most of the hour Lisa played uninterrupted, as the old man sat in silence, occasionally bringing his hand down to emphasize an accent in the music. Finally, he put down his music and just listened. She looked over and saw a distressed expression on his face. Was she playing that badly?

At the end of the piece, the professor made no comment. Lisa went on to her customary scales and waited anxiously for her assignment. The professor focused on scraping the bowl of his pipe into the ashtray.

"May I do the adagio for next week?" she asked nervously. She loved the second movement and yearned to show him her improving legato.

He looked at her for a long moment, then finally spoke, looking uncomfortable and ashamed: "I am sorry, Miss Jura. But I am required to tell you that I cannot continue to teach you."

Lisa was stunned and unable to move. The professor walked to his window and opened the curtain. He stared at the people in the street. "There is a new ordinance," he said slowly. "It is now a crime to teach a Jewish child." He continued mumbling under his breath, then added in despair, "Can you imagine!"

Lisa felt tears rising.

"I am not a brave man," he said softly. "I am so sorry."

He came over to the piano, lifted up her slender young hands, and held them in his grip. "You have a remarkable gift, Lisa, never forget that."

Through her tears, she watched the professor pick up a thin gold chain that lay on top of the piano. It held a tiny charm in the shape of a piano.

"It is not much, but perhaps it will help you to remember the music we shared here," he said softly, fastening the gold chain around her neck with trembling fingers.

She stared through her tears at the stacks of music, the picture of Liszt on the wall, and tried to memorize every detail. She was afraid she might never see them again. Gathering her composure, she thanked the professor and collected her things, then turned and fled.

The cold November wind sent a deep shiver through Lisa's slender body as she pulled her coat tight around her and waited for the next streetcar. German SS, storm troopers, were everywhere she looked. Were they all staring at her? She threw her head back and walked defiantly toward the approaching car, climbing onto the landing and grabbing the frozen pole tightly with her woolen mittens. Staring back at the huge building, she memorized the pattern of its beveled glass windows, the size of its portico, and the gleam of the bronze door handle, shining from the polish of thousands of handclasps. The professor waved sadly before disappearing from his window.

Why were Germans telling Austrians what they could or couldn't do? It wasn't fair, and why were the Austrians letting them? There must be an answer—there must be someone to blame.

The faces on the streetcar were staring at her with pity. She quickly yanked the hat off her head and covered her face, realizing she had been crying since she'd left the studio. She wouldn't give these horrible people the satisfaction of watching her.

The ride was endless, its magic gone. She couldn't wait to get back to Franzensbrückestrasse, where everyone in the old neighborhood knew her—the little girl who played the piano. The neighbors had gossiped at first about her mother, Malka, when she had bought that expensive upright piano from Mr. Minsky's secondhand store. How could the Juras afford it? Such an extravagant purchase in these tense times.

But five years later, the neighbors had realized their shortsightedness. Malka's daughter was special. She had a gift. You could hear it in the butcher's shop, you could hear it in the bakery—the music drifted everywhere. The street itself seemed to smile when the little girl played. People started calling her by that special word: Lisa Jura was a prodigy.

Sometimes Lisa played so loudly that her banging octaves could be heard above the clatter of the trashcans and mixed into the teeming loudness of tenement clatter.

But when she played softly and sweetly, old couples would move to their windows and stop whatever they were doing. Schubert and Mozart would float down the stairs, in and out of apartments, and fill the neighborhood with grace.

The music transported the mind of this precocious teenager into fanciful imaginings. As she played the first bars of a Strauss waltz, she saw herself in a satin ball gown, her hand held high by some count or marquis, being led to the dance floor. The elegant crowd parted as she made her entrance.

From the time she was a little girl, Malka taught Lisa to surrender herself completely to the music by telling her stories and painting fantastic images. For Lisa the music became her whole world: an escape from the dark streets, the rundown flats, shops, and markets that were home to Vienna's working-class Jews. And now, the most important escape of all, from the Nazis.

As she neared 13 Franzensbrückestrasse, Lisa's steps were uncharacteristically slow. Her heels barely left the ground; her upright posture sagged. She arrived in her living room and dropped her music on the bench with a gesture that alarmed her mother.

"What is it, Liseleh, what's wrong?" Malka took her daughter in her arms and stroked her hair. Lisa cried desperately. Malka guessed what must have happened. "Is it Professor Isseles?"

Lisa nodded.

"Don't worry, I taught you before. I will teach you again." Lisa tried to smile at her mother's offer, but they both knew that Lisa had long ago surpassed her mother's ability.

"Let's play something now. Let's begin the day all over again."

"I can't play now, Mama. I'm too upset."

"Oh, Lisa, have you forgotten all I've taught you? It's at times like this that your music is most important."

Malka went to the cupboard and pulled out the complete preludes by Chopin; after opening the book to the number four in E Minor, she sat at the piano.

"I'll play the right hand, you play the left," Malka insisted.

"I can't."

"Play what is in your heart."

Lisa sat beside her, playing the four-four rhythm of the marching, repeating chords. When she'd mastered the left hand, she took over from her mother, blending the plaintive melody of the upper register with the somber chords of the base. The melody reached its final question and found resolution in an exquisite pianissimo.

Outside, an old woman put down her heavy groceries, leaned against the building, and listened.

When she finished the Chopin, Lisa went to her room and lay down, crying as silently as possible into the pillow.

A few minutes later she felt a warm hand on her shoulder, stroking her gently. It was her older sister, Rosie. "Don't cry, Lisa," she urged. "Come on. I'll show you something."

Lisa finally rolled over and looked up at the smartly dressed twenty-year-old. She was always happy when her older sister made time for her, since Rosie had been spending most of her time these days with her fiancé, Leo.

"Crying won't help, Lisa. Let me show you something I just learned, come on," Rosie insisted, taking Lisa by the hand.

Lisa stumbled into the bathroom behind her sister and glimpsed her tearstained face in the mirror. Rosie emptied out the contents of a cloth bag and spread all manner of powder and paints on the bathroom dresser.

"I'll show you a new way to do your lips—you'll look just like Marlene Dietrich."

As they had so many times before, Rosie carefully applied lipstick and eye makeup to Lisa's face.

"See? A little bit wider than the lip line."

Her sister should know, Lisa thought. She had been the runner-up in a Miss Vienna contest—two years earlier—when they had still allowed non-Aryan contestants. Without warning, their twelve-year-old sister Sonia burst through the door.

"What are you two doing in here!"

"Look at Lisa, doesn't she look like a movie star?"

Lisa stared excitedly at her new face in the mirror. She looked five years older! The sound of footsteps approaching stopped them in their tracks.

"Quick! Mama's coming!"

In a well-rehearsed drill, Lisa scrubbed her face with soap and water and Rosie scrambled to hide the cosmetics, as little Sonia looked on and giggled. Rosie put a protective arm around Lisa, and for a moment the sorrow of Professor Isseles seemed far away. The three sisters joined hands and emerged to greet their mother.

2

ISA!" MALKA yelled from the kitchen. "Look out the window for your father."

Lisa rose reluctantly from the piano bench and went to the window of their second-story apartment, peering into the cobblestone courtyard.

"Do you see him?"

"No, Mama, not yet." The wind was blowing fiercely; the streetlights rattled. Winter was on its way. Before long, it would be Hanukkah, the Festival of Lights, Lisa's favorite time of year.

"Is he there yet?"

"No, I said I didn't see him!"

"Where is he!" Malka began making a lot of noise with the pans in the kitchen. It was her way of letting off steam.

"Don't break anything, Mama!" Lisa said, laughing.

She was answered with another crash. "All right, then, get your sisters and we'll start without him."

* * *

Lisa knew what was making her father late: It was that "gambling" thing her mother got so angry about. He would stay out playing cards with some of the neighborhood men in the storeroom of Mr. Rothbard's butcher shop. Lisa didn't understand a thing about cards, but she knew they must be terrible since they made her mother so upset.

Abraham Jura had always called himself "the best tailor in all Vienna." Her father was a proud, elegant man who wore starched white shirts with tall collars. His customers had been Jews and gentiles alike and came from all over the city to have their suits custom-made. But now Abraham had few sewing jobs, his longtime customers were turning up with less frequency. Gentiles had been forbidden to use Jewish tailors. A sign on his shop read *"Jüdisches Geschäft"*: *"Jewish Business."*

Sometimes, after she was in bed, there were raised voices coming from her parents' bedroom. The arguments were about money; that much she could figure out, and it seemed her father was angry at almost everyone these days. Gone were the early evening dinners and the bear hugs when Papa came home from work to greet his family.

She was upset by his wrinkled clothes and frayed cuffs. Fingering the loose buttons, she frowned. "Papa, I'm going to sew your buttons on for you. You must have forgotten how," she teased him playfully. "Who will come visit a tailor that has a loose button?"

Her father would look at her sadly and say nothing. At those times, when she felt her father changing before her eyes, she would escape to the piano and her fantasies.

Abraham or no Abraham, Malka lit the Shabbat candles. It was Friday sunset and the Sabbath was beginning. She lit two white tapers in the silver holders that had been

13

her own mother's and turned to her youngest daughter. "Sonia, why don't you tell us what they mean?"

"One candle is for the Lord, who made the heaven and the earth and rested on the seventh day," Sonia replied proudly.

"And the second candle, Lisa?"

"We light the second because we observe the Sabbath day and keep it holy."

Malka lit four more candles, one for each of her three daughters and one for her mother, Briendla, in Poland. A warm yellow light filled the room. A similar glow was appearing in parlors and dining rooms all across the neighborhood.

Lisa's mother had a tradition of feeding the poor on the night of the Sabbath, and people would line up in the hallway an hour before sunset. Some came in tattered clothing and unkempt hair, others came with neatly mended patches, temporarily down on their luck. The faces would change, but one remained the same—a tall old man with a straggly white beard, the girls' favorite, who told them a story every week.

This evening, rather than bringing a plate of hot kosher food, Malka came into the hallway and said sadly, "I am afraid we have nothing to share tonight."

Lisa was stunned. She watched the hungry people shuffle away and saw the sorrow in her mother's eyes. The old storyteller stayed behind, staring at the mezuzah hanging in the doorway.

After a long painful moment, he turned to Malka: "God will bless you for all of your past generosity."

The girls joined their mother inside and began the meal without their father. When they finished, they cleared the table and watched her pull the large mahogany rocking chair to the window. Malka rocked slowly back and forth, reciting her prayers, eyes focused on the street below.

Lisa and Sonia awoke to loud noises—not the usual raised voices that often accompanied her father's late night homecomings, but ominous noises of distant shouting.

Throwing on their robes, they rushed to her parents' bedroom. It was empty, so they ran to the living room window and saw the sky was red with the flames of burning buildings. Above the shouting came the piercing sound of shattering glass. It exploded in terrifying crescendos from up and down the streets. Storm troopers were running down the block like a band of outlaws—brown-shirted soldiers were throwing rocks and bricks through windows. They swung clubs recklessly in the air. She wondered if they were drunk. Did they let soldiers drink?

Even though it was late, dozens of neighbors ran out onto the street. Lisa saw Mr. Mendelsohn, the druggist, racing out of his building, and watched in horror as two SS men picked him off the ground, flinging him into the plate-glass window of the pharmacy. She heard his agonized screams, jerked Sonia away from the window, and pulled her little sister back into the bedroom they shared. "Get under the bed and stay there." Sonia looked up imploringly. "Get under the bed!" Lisa yelled, and ran into the hallway to search for her mother.

"Lisa!" She heard the cry on the stairwell and ran down to find her mother holding her father's head in her lap. His face was covered with blood; his clothes were torn.

"It's only a small cut, Lisa, don't worry," her father said when he saw her terrified expression.

"Are you all right? Where is Sonia? Where is Rosie?"

"I sent Sonja to hide under the bed, Rosie said she was going to Leo's, remember? Let me help you with Papa."

She took one elbow and her mother took the other, and they walked him slowly upstairs. As she looked back out the front door, she saw dozens of people being shoved down the road and beaten by soldiers.

Malka and Abraham had a beautiful bed, carved from cherrywood polished to a glow. Malka prized the bed above all other possessions. The children were never allowed to sit on the delicate white satin sheets, which had belonged to Malka's grandmother. Now, as they helped Abraham onto the bed, Malka ignored the blood that stained the sheets and cleaned his cuts with a warm towel.

Lisa gently picked the shards of glass out of the folds of his clothing as her father chanted the Shema, the ancient prayer of the Jewish people.

"*Shema Yisrael, Adonai Eloheinu, Adonai Echad.*": "Hear O Israel, the Lord our God, the Lord is One." When he had finally calmed down, he began to speak.

"I was leaving Rothbard's when I saw them. I knew something was wrong—they weren't marching any-where—they were a mob. They took turns smashing the windows, the biggest ones first, like it was fun for them—they enjoyed the noise. Then they wrote nasty words in paint."

"What kinds of words, Papa?"

"Shh," Malka said. "We don't need to know."

"She'll see them soon enough. They said *Juden! Juden Schwein!* Kill the Jews. Then one of them threw a bottle with gasoline inside a building." Lisa was riveted by her father's terrifying words.

Malka finished wiping Abraham's face. "Shh, now. Let's get you some soup." But Abraham continued.

"I saw them drag people out of their homes. They took their things and burned them. Children that came into the streets were thrown on the ground. It was good you stayed inside."

"Don't tell us any more, Abraham."

"You need to know what I saw! When I was running past the synagogue, they were taking out the ark and throwing the scrolls and the Torah in the street and setting them on fire . . . they were burning the Torah in the street!"

He paused to take a breath. "And there were no sirens. They wanted everything to burn."

"I'll turn on the radio, Papa, maybe there is news. Maybe the chancellor is saying something." Lisa ran into the living room and twisted the large knob of the wireless; a stream of German patriotic music emerged. Abraham came into the room, walking gingerly in bare feet, trying to avoid loose pieces of glass, and switched off the radio.

More screams came from the window. They ran over and saw flames shooting out of the house on the corner and the neighbors were forming a bucket brigade. Men were running into the streets with pails.

"Malka, I need my shoes!"

She said nothing but walked into the bedroom and brought her husband his heavy boots. He laced them up in seconds and ran down the stairs to help.

The frightened family stared out the window. They watched the bonfires grow larger as more and more books and possessions were added to the fires.

Suddenly, several storm troopers grabbed the men from the bucket brigade and dragged them into the street. Lisa watched in horror as her father was forced to strip naked, get down on his knees, and scrub the dirty pavement. The storm troopers yelled, *"Schwein, Juden Schwein!"* and kicked them when they didn't move fast enough.

Malka could no longer bear the shame. She took her two girls by the hand and led them to the bedroom, where they waited in silence for the terrible night to end.

3

HERE WERE curfews now. Jews were not allowed on the streets at night or in movie theaters, concert halls, or most public places.

Nazi cruelties had continued. Soldiers kept up their attacks on stores and homes, and beatings in the street became a common sight. Storm troopers broke into homes and arrested many of the men. It was whispered that they were being taken away to prison camps.

Abraham's tailor shop on the first floor was now closed by government order. A poster covered the cracked glass of the storefront window. Someone had tried to scratch out the letters, but it could still be read: *"Judenblut, Schweinblut!"*

Twelve-year-old Sonia could not understand why all of this was happening. She still went to school, but the Jewish children had been separated from the gentiles. She was not allowed to talk to any of her friends who weren't Jewish. The day her best friend stopped speaking to her Sonia came home crying.

"Why, Mama, why?" she sobbed.

Malka tried to find an answer, but she had trouble understanding it herself.

"Do you remember the Purim story about Queen Esther and Haman?" she asked, holding Sonia.

The girl nodded.

"Haman was the evil adviser to King Ahasuerus very long ago and wanted to kill all the Jews. But the king fell in love with Esther, who was a Jew herself and very beautiful, so he married her and made her the queen. Esther then used her royal power to save all the Jews."

"I remember," Sonia said.

"So now," Malka continued, "there is an evil man who is just like Haman; his name is Adolf Hitler. He is as evil as Haman, but he can't hurt us if we are brave and act wisely. We must have faith. The Jews are a people chosen by God. If we keep believing in God, He will protect us."

Malka kissed her younger daughter, then got up and went to the piano. "Come, Liseleh, let's work on the 'Clair de Lune.'" Lisa pulled a worn folio of sheet music from the pile and put Debussy's masterpiece on top of the piano.

"Close your eyes for a moment before you begin. Where do you see yourself?"

"On a desert island. Across the ocean," Lisa answered without hesitation.

"Can I go, too?" Sonia chimed in, shutting her eyes tightly.

"Of course you can," her mother answered lovingly.

Lisa opened her eyes brightly and placed her fingers on the keys. The music shimmered softly like the moonlight bouncing off the waters of a distant ocean. Looking up from the keyboard, she saw her mother close her eyes and smile. Malka's head began to sway as she was transported on the waves of her daughter's silvery tones.

Malka had begged her husband not to go out, but he'd refused. "If you are caught, what will we do?" Malka had pleaded. "Mr. Stern next door didn't come back last night!"

"I can't stay inside all the time, I'll go mad!" He had gathered his coat and left hurriedly, afraid to look his wife in the eye. He had gone out into the streets, pitch black since the smashing of the streetlights.

It was late when he returned.

Lisa strained to hear snatches of their conversation. "We must do something immediately. The chance may not come again."

Lisa crept out of bed and stood in the hallway. She heard the words *Holland* and *England*.

"They are not letting Jews out of Vienna," her father continued. "But they are allowing some trains to take Jewish children. Hundreds have already gone. Parents are fighting—they're begging for a spot on the trains. It's what everyone is talking about."

"Children are going away without their parents?" Her mother's voice was weak and frightened. "Where are they going?"

"England. Trains are being organized to take them to England. I think we have to consider this."

"Listen to what you're saying. Send the children without us! Without their family!"

"My cousins Dora and Sid live in London. This could be our only chance."

"Things will surely get better, Abraham. Things can't be so bad. We must have faith."

"Malka, there is chaos at the Kultusgemeinde. I hear such terrible stories, I cannot bear to tell them to you. Please trust me. We must do it!"

"How could we do it even if we wanted?"

"Let me finish. Mr. Rothbard said that his wife refuses under any condition to send their son on the train, he thinks the whole family can get out another way. We don't have such a way. We can't stay together right now. He will give the son's place to us."

Malka drew in her breath with surprise and anguish. "So you are asking me to send my precious daughters away?"

"Malka, you must hear me, he has only one place, for only one child right now. We must send Lisa or Sonia . . . Rosie is over eighteen, she isn't eligible." Abraham's voice was wretchedly unhappy.

Lisa heard her mother start to cry.

"How could we do this? How could we bear it?"

Abraham pleaded, "One of our daughters can be safe. As soon as we are able, we will find a way to send the others. . . ."

"It can't be the time for this. It can't be," Malka whispered in disbelief.

Lisa heard her mother's footsteps as she emerged from the kitchen. Malka smiled sadly at her daughter. "Go to bed now, my darling. Go to bed."

She kissed her mother's cheek and walked into the bedroom, where Sonia was sleeping peacefully next to her rag dolls. Lisa stared at her sister and wondered what the decision would be.

*　　*　　*

The next morning Lisa was reading at the kitchen table when her parents entered the room. Abraham stared at the beautiful fourteen-year-old who had inherited his red hair, his winning smile, and the same solid resolve.

"We have made a decision," her mother said. "We are sending you to England. We would like to send all of you, but we are forced to choose only one. You are strong, Lisa. You are strong and you have your music to guide you. . . . We will send you first. As soon as we can find enough money, we will send your sisters." Then Malka began to cry.

Lisa was silent, and although she felt like crying herself, she wouldn't give in to her tears. It would be harder for her mother if she cried. She forced herself to push aside the images of good-byes and separation that flooded her mind.

"Where will I go? What will I do there?" She didn't quite understand how she would live on her own but wasn't sure that her parents had the answers, either. She would do what her mother had told her. She would have faith.

"There is an organization called the Bloomsbury House, that has arranged for Jewish children to come to England. It's safer there," said her father.

"Can't we go together? Can't we wait and go together?"

Abraham looked tenderly at his daughter. "Sonia will come next, and then Rosie and Leo and your mother and I will join you. Your cousins will take care of you until we get there."

"Who are these cousins?" Lisa asked, forlorn.

"My aunt's cousins. I have never met them, but I am told one is also a tailor. A tailor in London."

Lisa forced herself to conjure up the image of a handsome man in an elegant suit and hat. "Then I will work for him and send you the money, you'll see."

That Sunday, it was unseasonably warm and the family decided to have a picnic. Lisa and Sonia wore tailored dresses that their father had made, while Rosie chose a fashionable wraparound with the latest-style cape collar. Leo helped Malka carry the basket, which was packed tightly with meats and fancy foods that were a treat after weeks of thin soups and rough breads. They didn't go to the Prater as they had in other times; the sign on the heavy metal gates was clear: *"Juden Verboten"*: "No Jews." They walked instead to a tram stop for the ride to the Vienna woods. It was the family's favorite summer picnic spot, but they had never gone in winter. When the tram finally arrived, a new sign had been added. *"Juden und Hunden Verboten"*: "No Jews or Dogs."

They walked back silently to the apartment. Malka spread the tablecloth on the back landing overlooking the courtyard. A neighbor saw them and waved. "Nice day for a picnic!"

"You could not ask for better," Malka answered, trying to add cheer to her voice.

Abraham suddenly hummed the oompah-pah phrase of the Ferris wheel music from the Prater. Malka smiled and whistled along, and Lisa yelled: "Here comes the marching band!" and banged a rat-a-tat on the plate with her knife.

Sonia caught on and waved her arms in the air. "Look at me. I'm leading the band. Look at me!"

The family laughed and sang almost as they had in better years, when Vienna was still the old Vienna and they had not been forced to inhabit its new dark universe.

*   *   *

The Kindertransport was set to leave the week after Hanukkah, although no one knew exactly what day. The family lit the menorah each night and said their prayers. No friends came by since Jews were no longer allowed on the streets without a special pass. Still, there was joy because the family was together.

Lisa's bag had been packed for several days. She would take only one small suitcase—enough to hold a change of clothes and her good Shabbat dress. She knew she would have little room on the train.

Then, one night, Abraham got the call: Lisa's train would be leaving the following morning. From her bed, she overheard her father's conversation. She had thought about this moment every day since the decision had been made. She had prepared for it; it had overwhelmed everything else in her mind. Yet when the call actually came, it took her by surprise.

Bathed in tears, she lay in her bed and with gentle motions stroked the stitching of her mother's embroidered sheets. How long until she would sleep under them again? How long until she would be reunited with her loving family?

She awoke before anyone else and laid out her blue twill coat with its matching checkered scarf. She stood at the mirror and put on the little felt hat with the blue ribbon, adjusting it to the perfect tilt.

She walked through the house, determined to remember everything she loved, yet already feeling like a stranger. She scanned the walls, counted the paintings, and fingered the beautiful bone lace across the dining table. Gently, she touched the blue-and-white porcelain figure of an old tailor, which her father had brought from

Dresden years ago, and leafed through the worn leather scrapbook of hand-tinted postcards.

Then she stopped at the piano and brushed her fingers in the air above the keys. The copy of "Clair de Lune" was on the piano. Guiltily she rolled it up and put it in her pocket. It was a silly luxury, she thought, since she had so little space, but she couldn't help herself.

Her mother came in from the hall and put on her heavy coat. "It's time to go."

"Mama, will you promise me something?"

Malka smiled at her daughter. "Of course."

"Will you promise me that you won't move anything in this room? That you will leave it all just as it is? I want to know it's still like this when I think about it," Lisa whispered so quietly that her mother could barely hear her.

"I promise, Liseleh." Malka smiled back at her, then took her daughter in her arms and rocked her.

The Westbahnhof station was overflowing with people; Lisa had never seen it so crowded. Hundreds of desperate families rubbed shoulder to shoulder in panic and confusion, and pushed belongings of all shapes and sizes toward the waiting train. At the door to each car Nazi soldiers in long brown coats shouted into bullhorns as they inspected suitcases and documents.

When the crowd became too dense, the Jura family stopped for their final good-byes. It had been decided that Rosie, Sonia, and Abraham would say good-bye first, then Lisa's mother would walk her to the train. Abraham had been carrying the small suitcase for his daughter. When he stopped and handed it to her, Lisa could only clutch the handle and stand frozen. She felt that if anyone moved from her side, she would fall to pieces like a broken china figurine.

Abraham put his arm around Rosie, easing her toward Lisa, and the two sisters embraced. "Don't forget to take the window seat so we can see you," her beautiful older sister shouted above the noise. "We'll all be together again soon, be brave for us."

Next, Abraham gently pushed his youngest daughter forward. Lisa kissed her, reached into her pocket, and slipped Professor Isscles's tiny gold charm around Sonia's neck. "Close your eyes and picture all of us together soon . . . and keep this for me until I see you again. . . ."

Then Abraham took Lisa in a hug so tight that neither one could breathe. He was crying, something she could never remember seeing him do before, not even on Kristallnacht. Finally, Malka took her hand and guided her through the crowd toward the platform.

The children were lined up, waiting their turn to board. Some of them were Lisa's age, some older, some younger, carrying their cherished toys and dolls. Teary-eyed parents buttoned their coats, brushed their hair, and laced up untied shoes.

"You be on your best behavior. . . ."

"Don't forget to eat your lunch. . . ."

"Don't take your sweater off; you'll catch a cold. . . ."

In front of Lisa and her mother was a little boy of about ten. Along with his suitcase he carried a large red accordion. "You'll have to leave this here," said the guard. "No valuables are to leave the country."

"It's not that valuable," protested the boy. "I need it to practice."

"Show me that you can play it," insisted the guard.

The boy sat down his bag and strapped on the accor-

27

dion. His head was barely visible behind the huge instrument. He began to play a simple polka—his hands shaking from fear. Its unexpected three-four beat drifted down the platform and for an eerie moment, the clatter of the crowd stopped, as they listened. The guard stared, then motioned for the boy to move forward with his instrument as the clamor of good-byes began again.

Malka looked at her daughter, who was next in line, and held her close. "You must make me a promise."

"What is it, Mama?"

"You must promise me . . . that you will hold on to your music. Please promise me that."

"How can I?" Lisa sobbed. "How can I without you?" She dropped her little suitcase and embraced her mother tightly.

"You can and you will. Remember what I've taught you. Your music will help you through—let it be your best friend, Liseleh. And remember that I love you."

"Move forward now," the guard commanded, and waved Lisa up the steep metal stairs. At that moment Malka slipped a little card into her daughter's hand. Lisa didn't even have a chance to glance at it: Before she knew it, she was separated from her mother and carried along onto the train car.

Pushed up the steps and swept down the long corridor, Lisa moved quickly to a seat by the window. The glass was covered by the condensation of many fevered breaths, and she furiously wiped a patch clear with the sleeve of her coat. She watched as children were wrenched bodily from their mothers and shoved onto the train. Trembling, she searched for her mother's dark hair and black coat. She thought she could see her and waved frantically, but she did not know whether her mother could pick her out.

She yelled through the glass, "Mama!" but her voice was lost in a chorus of similar cries.

Finally there was a low clank releasing the brakes, and the train began to move. For a moment she thought she could make out her family, pushed behind a barricade, waving faithfully. Then everything disappeared into the steam and the smoke.

She looked down for the first time at the envelope she clutched in her hand—the last thing her mother had given her. She tore it open and inside found a photograph of Malka standing straight and proud, taken on the day of Lisa's last recital at school. On the back was written, *"Fon diene nicht fergesene mutter"*: "So you will never forget your mother."

The train gathered speed, and the buildings passed in a blur. The snowy fields came into view and the city shrank into the distance. She stared and stared at the disappearing skyline. Finally the giant silhouette of the Ferris wheel was the only landmark visible—turning slowly above the white roofline of Vienna.

4

$\mathcal{L}$ ISA STUDIED the faces of the other children, hoping to see someone from her school, from her neighborhood, from her synagogue. Yet the train was filled with strangers.

Some of them were crying; others sat quietly. Each had his or her little suitcase, his or her pack of food. There was a tag around each child's neck. Lisa was number 158. What a boring, stupid number, she thought, completely unmemorable. How high did the numbers go? she wondered. Are there a thousand of us? Where will we all go? Where will I go?

A couple of five-year-old girls sat across from Lisa, sharing an orange tea cake among them and giggling stupidly. They acted as though they were going on holiday.

A boy of eleven with freckles and round red cheeks sat next to her. He was nervous and eager.

"I'm Michael," he said matter-of-factly. He fussed in his bags and offered up a smelly paper sack.

"Would you like half of my sardine sandwich?" he asked politely. "I don't mind sharing."

"Thank you, no," she said curtly. She felt hemmed in by his forward behavior and his pleasant mood. There is no room on this tiny train seat for two, she thought, but was afraid to say so. Why was he so happy? She didn't want anything to do with him—or with any of these children, now that she thought about it. She wanted to be alone with the thoughts of her family. She wanted to continue to memorize every inch of the existence she was leaving. She couldn't take the chance of forgetting the slightest detail.

"I can't wait to get to London!" he blurted. The boy would not give up. "I've read all of Sherlock Holmes and I'm going to see his home on Baker Street. I'm going to be a great detective when I grow up. What are you going to be?"

Lisa sighed her most unapproachable sigh.

"I know. I bet you'll be a rich man's wife and have lots of children."

"I am a pianist. I will play music," she said, unable to keep to her plan of aloofness.

"Wow," he said, genuinely impressed. "What kind of music?"

"The music my mother taught me," Lisa answered grandly. "The great music of Vienna."

Suddenly all Lisa could think about was her mother, her poor mother. She heard the terrible sound of the breaking glass of Kristallnacht ring inside her head. She shut her eyes tightly, but the sound wouldn't go away. What if another Kristallnacht came, would her family be safe?

When she opened her eyes, she was confronted again by the absurd smile on the face of the boy next to her. She hated him.

"London will be wonderful!" he insisted.

"You don't know anything about London!" Lisa exploded. "You've never been there. You're not a detective in a book, you know. You are a refugee!"

Michael looked at her. A dark mood overtook his face.

She closed her eyes again and went back to her thoughts.

But Michael began again; his tone was different, and there were tears in his eyes. "My father told me . . . that I should only think about what I love the most and . . . it, it will come true when I get to England." His lip trembled.

Lisa opened her eyes and looked at him. "I'm sorry," she said. "I didn't mean it."

Michael kept crying.

"Please don't cry," she begged. "Forget what I said. Tell me what else you know about London."

"London is the most marvelous city! The fog is thick and fills the air, and evil spies lurk around every corner, while master criminals prowl the underground stations!"

Lisa looked at him coquettishly. "No! Really?"

Several of the younger children near them climbed from their seats and huddled around Michael. He rambled and raved about Jack the Ripper and blood-curdling adventures. Lisa felt her eyelids grow heavy, and soon the monotonous rhythm of the train put her to sleep.

She woke to the sound of rustling beside her. Michael was digging frantically through his small suitcase. The lights in the car had been dimmed and most everyone near them was asleep.

"What are you doing?" she whispered.

"The train is stopping," said Michael. "I saw SS soldiers out the window."

"So?" she asked, still groggy from sleep.

He didn't answer; he had found what he was looking for. He pulled a small leather drawstring bag out of the case on his lap and opened it, revealing a tiny pearl necklace, a silver bracelet, and a pocketwatch with a reddish gold chain.

"These belonged to my parents," he said nervously. His voice was shaking. "But if the soldiers find them, they'll take them away and send me back."

"Really, they would send you back?"

Michael didn't answer; he stuffed the jewelry back into the sack and stood up on the seat. He climbed onto the armrest, yanked down the heavy train window, and shook the contents of the bag out into the night. Lisa gasped and reached up after him but stopped herself; perhaps this was the right thing to do, she thought. She didn't know what was the right thing to do anymore! She watched the brief flash of light as the gold and silver vanished into the night.

The train groaned to a halt and Michael sank into his chair, paralyzed by the enormity of what he had done. The engine let out a gasp of steam and jerked still. The children around them awakened and everyone, even the youngest children, sat eerily still, watching the long-coated soldiers move through the car.

Lisa examined their uniforms and their demeanors. They were identical to the soldiers who had marched through her streets. Her mood sank lower as she realized that these men were everywhere, not just in Vienna.

The Nazis came up the aisle, pushing, prying, and poking into bags. They shook toys and rummaged through lunches. A young child began wailing and someone put a hand across his mouth.

Michael leaned toward Lisa, his forehead dripping with

sweat. His whisper was choked with panic. "Maybe they saw me!"

Lisa put her finger to her lips and hissed a forceful, "Shush!"

The guard approached and looked at Michael closely. The boy's knees were shaking uncontrollably. "What is your name!" the guard shouted.

"Muh, Michael Liebel." He fingered his tag and turned it toward the guard. Number 38. The guard moved on, never glancing at the suitcase on the boy's lap.

After a while the heavy doors of the train closed, and the SS left the transport. The engines groaned again, and Michael started to sob. "I threw it all away for nothing! For nothing! I'm so stupid!"

Lisa placed her arm on his shoulder tenderly. "What you did was very brave."

"No! I was stupid! That was my father's watch, the one his father gave him!"

"Stop crying! You'll be a famous detective and buy him a nicer watch, you'll see! Let's do a little something my mother taught me. Whenever I begin a new piece of music, she has me close my eyes and imagine a wonderful place. It's very important. Let's close our eyes really tight and imagine the new places we are going to see, all right? Ready?"

Michael regained his composure, and together they closed their eyes.

"Go."

The two children sat with their eyes closed for a long time. Lisa opened hers first. "All right, you can open them. . . . So what did you see?"

"Nothing," he said. "I couldn't see anything at all."

"Me neither," she said softly. "Oh, dear. I wonder where we really are going."

Michael smiled at her, and she laid her head against his shoulder. They tried to sleep.

The train stopped several times in the night, and more and more children got on. The newcomers were packed into the aisles and sat wedged on top of their suitcases. There must be fifty of us in this car alone! thought Lisa. Michael offered his seat to a pretty German girl Lisa's age and went off up the aisle. She watched him staring out the window, fingering his leather jewelry bag.

"Did you see the handsome one over there?" the new girl asked. "He's been eyeing me ever since we got on."

"No, he wasn't, Mela!" the friend snapped.

Both girls were vivacious and attractive, dressed in dark, stylish skirts and crisp white blouses. They turned to Lisa. "Look down the aisle. . . . Which one of us was he staring at?"

The idea of watching out for boys struck her as ridiculous under the circumstances. How shallow they are, Lisa thought, but soon she found herself stretching her neck to look down the aisle. "Which one?"

"Over there, silly! Quick, or he'll know we're looking!"

The handsome boy looked up, smiled, and winked at his admirers. The two new girls dissolved into giggles. Lisa couldn't help herself. She laughed along with them.

So *what's wrong with having fun?* the voice inside her chided. *If Rosie were here, she'd lead the way. And if Sonia were here* . . . Sonia. Why couldn't she have come, too? she asked herself. Why did I get the new life and not her? Oh, Sonia, I miss you.

The new girls practiced their English. "Shall I fetch you tea?" Helen asked.

"Two lumps!" answered the other, Mela, with a diction that Lisa would have died for. She had tried to prepare herself by studying an English primer she'd bought in the temple bazaar, but two weeks had not been enough time. She hated that she was going to arrive in England, open her mouth, and sound like a refugee.

"Would you like some tea?" Lisa uttered to herself over and over, silently imitating the pleasant tones of the other girls.

The train was starting up again; the guards had slammed the doors. As the children prepared for another departure, there was a loud rapping against one of the windows. An older boy climbed up and lowered it to see what was happening. As the train lurched forward, a wicker laundry basket was thrust into the boy's arms.

"Somebody's brought us hot muffins!"

"Maybe it's chocolate!"

"I bet it's cheese."

"What if it's a bomb?" one girl chimed in.

Everyone froze. The boy put the basket in the aisle and moved away from it.

"I dare you to open it," a boy bullied his seatmate.

"Not me, stupid, you open it."

"Maybe we should throw it back."

Lisa had an odd feeling she could not explain, a certainty about something. She walked up the aisle and stood over the basket, thinking, If I'm afraid of this, I'll be afraid of everything new. I won't let myself be afraid, I won't. She opened the lid.

Before her lay a beautiful baby, wrapped in a clean blanket and sound asleep. A little angel. She picked it up gently and cradled it. The older girls rushed to Lisa's side while the boys stood back. The car erupted in debate.

"What should we do with it?"

"Does it have a tag?"

"Do you think it's hungry?"

The baby started to cry, and someone panicked. "If they hear it, we'll all be thrown off." Lisa immediately began to hum a Brahm's lullaby—the first melody that she could think of.

But the infant continued to cry. Its wails got louder, and the children became more nervous. Lisa sang desperately to quiet the child, but to no avail.

From up the aisle a sixteen-year-old girl came and held out her arms. "I have a little brother at home. Let me try."

The girl took the child expertly and nestled her nose into its flesh. It smiled for a second. The entire car breathed a sigh of relief.

When the infant's crying stopped, she eased him back into the basket and joined Lisa in scouring the car for juice, milk, and blankets. They took turns rocking and feeding the new baby. At that moment, it seemed to Lisa that everyone in the car shared a common purpose.

Lisa felt a growing sense of determination. If I can keep strong, she thought, I can make it. I'll make it for Mama and I'll make it for Papa. And soon we will all be together again.

A long, shrill whistle sounded and the train stopped again. The children hid the juice and the blankets and pushed the basket under Lisa's seat. Someone saw a sign out the window.

"It's in Dutch! The sign is in Dutch! We must be at the border!" A hush fell over them.

A stony-faced SS officer made his way down the aisle for a final inspection, pushing aside suitcases to make way for his shiny black boots. He checked names and numbers off a list on his clipboard.

When the guard stopped at Lisa's row, everyone held their breath. Several children began nervous conversations to cover the awkward silence that had fallen over the railroad car. The guard opened the lid of the basket and saw the sleeping baby. He stared at it for what seemed an interminable moment, then looked at his list.

"Isn't he sweet?" Lisa asked, interrupting him. And she smiled brilliantly, praying it would distract him. She put every ounce of charm she had into that smile. He turned and looked at her for a long moment, and finally, without uttering a word, moved on, making his way briskly down the aisle. He opened the heavy doors at the end of the car and disappeared into the next carriage.

As the Kindertransport crossed the border into Holland, the lights inside the car came on for the first time, and cheers erupted. Lisa opened the basket and stared at the helpless bundle. "No one can hurt you now," she whispered.

It was a bright, moonlit night. Through the window she saw the windmills turning slowly—like in the picture books Papa had shown her. The Chopin Nocturne in E Minor, calming and elegant, ran through her mind. The wooden arms of the windmills moved with the rhythm of the music.

They arrived at the Hook of Holland, the port on the North Sea. The train stopped, and an excited flock of round-cheeked Dutch women fluttered on board, carrying baskets filled with fat slices of fresh-baked bread and butter and big doughy cookies. One lady balanced a tray of steaming mugs of cocoa. The children forgot their manners and charged forward—shouting, "Me! Me!" as they devoured the treats. The Dutch women smiled at these faces smeared with chocolate.

There was discussion among the women about the baby boy. A serious-looking man with a red armband came up and introduced himself. He was from the Dutch Red Cross.

A group of girls gathered around the baby and watched as he directed a Dutch woman to pick up the infant from its basket. She held it snugly to her chest.

"We will find him a good home here," said the man.

"How will his parents know where to find him?" Lisa asked.

"I don't know."

Lisa picked up the wicker hamper and handed it to him. "Please take the basket," she begged. "Maybe someday someone will recognize it. Please keep the basket with him."

The man smiled sadly. "Yes, of course," he said, and took both the baby and basket with him.

The children emerged shyly from the train compartments and were led through the small station and across the large busy road to the seaport. When they realized there were no Nazi guards to keep them in line, some of the boys began to skip and play and trip the younger children around them.

Lisa ignored the scuffling of the silly boys and looked up at the loud cawing of a seagull above her head. The smell of the sea air, crisp and cool, raised her spirits.

Michael came rushing back from the head of the line

toward her. "I saw the boat, it's a real corker! Hurry up!" he screamed excitedly.

"What do you mean, a corker?" she asked.

"That's what Dr. Watson says about everything, what a corker! A corker is, well, something like that!" said Michael, pointing to the giant black cargo ship. "How does that stay afloat? It's made of metal!"

A bearded old seaman in a stiff green peacoat smiled and waved them along the dock toward the ramp. "Hurry along and up. Next stop is England." He sang out, "You'll cross the sea tonight, ye will, ye'll cross the sea tonight! You'll cross by moon and stars, ye will, by star and moonlight's bright."

Halfway up the ramp, Lisa stopped and looked back at the serene Dutch town with its orderly rows of thatched roofs. It didn't look the least bit like Vienna. Where will we end up? she asked herself. Will there be an opera house? Will there be a tower like St. Stephen's? No time for such thoughts, she told herself, and headed aboard.

She was assigned the top bunk above a whiny fifteen-year-old from Cologne who proudly announced that she was seasick and proved it by vomiting into her pillow.

Lisa lay awake for what seemed like hours, and looked out of the tiny porthole next to her bunk. The moon had disappeared and it was impossible to tell anymore where the water ended and the sky began. Eventually, the steady rising and falling of the sea caught up with her and she succumbed to a troubled sleep.

She dreamed of her home on Franzenbrückestrasse. Everything was just as she had left it: the paintings, the lace, the porcelain figurines. Her mother had kept her promise—nothing was changed. The family was just sitting down to dinner. Mama was serving her brisket, Papa was at the head of the table, ready to carve. Sonia was there, noisy and impatient, and so was Rosie, stately and beautiful. One chair was empty. "Where is Lisa?" her father asked. From deep inside her sleep, Lisa tried to respond.

"Here I am," she cried, but no one heard her; waves of green water drowned out her voice.

By morning they reached the other side of the English Channel. It was gray and cloudy as the single-file line of children walked down the gangplank. They clutched their little suitcases so tightly, one would have thought they carried their hearts inside.

A wiry man with a dark blue coat and a walrus mustache hurried them along. "There's a train to catch, let's look lively. Hurry along, luvs."

The single-file line wound through the center of the tiny English village—looping around the quaint central square and into the train station. It was dawn and no one was up but the milkman. He stared at the eerie sight of more than two hundred children winding through his town. Lisa thought they must have looked like a lost school field trip.

She turned to stare at the vast sea that separated her from her family and all she had ever known.

5

$\mathcal{T}$HE TRAIN rumbled through the English countryside past cows and hayfields, hedgerows and country lanes. The weary children collapsed onto one another, heads upon shoulders, their tiny, loose legs dangling with the swaying of the train.

Soon the winter pastures gave way to suburbs, and the suburbs gave way to stone buildings, and the journey reached its destination—Liverpool station, London.

Lisa and the two hundred exhausted children were met by a small battalion of well-wishers—nuns, rabbis, Quakers, clergy of every denomination, and Red Cross workers with clipboards. The new arrivals were lined up in the reception hall, sorted, and checked against the meticulously organized lists that had been prepared by the Jewish Refugee Agency at the Bloomsbury House. With a "Welcome to England, children, we're delighted to have you," the Red Cross workers moved down the line. Lisa waited anxiously and looked up at the huge windows of the cavernous structure as they extended to the ceiling to meet a massive glass dome, which filtered bright morning light onto people below. Finally, Lisa showed her papers and number and was relieved to see her name on the list.

A little girl next to her, five years old and teary eyed, hung on to Lisa's skirt. "Is my mommy going to be here? I want to see my mommy!" The girl began to cry inconsolably, and a volunteer came over, knelt down, and held her hand while they waited.

When the lists were completely checked and each child accounted for, barricades were opened and a stream of excited people holding photos flooded in. Some had signs—"Kaplan." "Samuel," "Friedler." They headed for the lines of waiting faces and yelled out names. "Ruthie Goldstein!" "Martin Muller!"

Lisa caught sight of Michael down the line and waved. He waved back, and then she watched as a man and woman in floor-length fur coats came up and hugged him, swallowing him up in their furry effusiveness.

The wait seemed interminable. Lisa held the handle of her suitcase and watched patiently as half the children departed in a flurry of handshakes and kisses. After what seemed like hours, she broke ranks and went up to a Red Cross worker who was handing out cookies. "Jura, Lisa Jura," she began, but that was as far as she got. She wanted to say, "My cousins are coming to get me," but suddenly couldn't remember the English words she had memorized so carefully.

"Be patient, dear, these things take time. Better get back in line so they can find you."

"*Muss ich zurück?*" Lisa asked, panicking. "Do we have to go back?" She suddenly imagined having to get on the train and go back if no one met her.

The Red Cross worker looked at her terrified face. "Of course not! *Zurück nicht*," the lady said in heavily anglicized German. "Don't worry, even if there's no one to meet you, we will take you to a very nice place. Let's get back in line . . . there's a good girl." She was leading Lisa back in line when a small man in a worn brown overcoat, holding a photo, came up and spoke to her in Yiddish.

"Lisa Jura? I'm your father's cousin, Sid Danziger."

Lisa expected that he would hug her, but he hung back, bowed his head slightly, and handed her some English treats. He asked about her family and consoled her as she spoke rapidly about the awful state of things in Vienna.

Then he cleared his throat and continued. "I'm afraid I have some bad news." He spoke so quietly, she could hardly hear him above the din.

"I'm afraid we've had to move outside London. My wife just had a baby, so we're leaving the city, and well, we're moving to a one-room flat, you see. There just isn't enough room. We won't be able to take you; we're very sorry." The man's face was flushed with embarrassment.

Lisa didn't know what to say. These were her relatives, her cousins, the only people that knew her in all of England.

When Sid saw the utter terror on her face, he stammered, "Please don't worry, I personally spoke to the people at Bloomsbury to make sure a good spot is found for you . . . and the main thing is that you are here in England."

Lisa couldn't hear all his words. Panic set in again. "But what about Sonia?" Her voice was frantic. She had fantasized that she could convince them to take her little sister as well.

"We'll do our best to ask our friends. We're not wealthy people, I'm sorry."

Lisa steeled herself against the disappointment. Mama would have wanted her to be polite. "Thank you for coming to sign for me," she managed.

"It's the least I could do," Sid replied sadly, and turned and walked away.

Lisa didn't speak during the ride from Liverpool station to the Bloomsbury House. She was wedged in the huge coach with the rest of the unclaimed children; there were dozens and dozens of them. She stared out the window at the bustle of London streets. What a hurried city! Horns honked, black taxis weaved in between double-decker buses—what a contrast to the placid pace of Vienna.

The Bloomsbury House that her father had spoken so much about was a massive stone building in London's West End. Getting off the bus, she saw Englishmen in pinstriped suits and shiny bowler hats walk by, looking just like the pictures she had seen in her schoolbooks.

She climbed the imposing stairs and sat with the others in the hallways. Children were everywhere. The phones were ringing shrilly, and people were shouting in languages she didn't understand. Occasionally someone yelled in Yiddish or German, and she smiled. But mainly it was the buzz of unfamiliar sounds. It reminded her of the tale that the old storyteller who used to visit in on Shabbes had told about the Tower of Babel—about the arrogance of mankind wanting to build a tower so tall that it would reach all the way to heaven—and how God had punished man by making him speak in different languages so people wouldn't understand each other. Yes, someone was punishing them, she thought. She just wished she could understand why.

Names were called, and one by one children went into an office for an interview. Women circulated with trays of sandwiches. Lisa was amused that anyone would put cucumbers on bread and forget the meat, but they tasted good anyway.

"Jura, Lisa Jura," a voice called, and she was waved politely into a small office. The tall and balding man behind the desk peered over his glasses and motioned for her to take a seat. Stacks upon stacks of papers in no discernible order covered the desk and spilled onto the floor.

"I'm Alfred Hardesty, nice to meet you."

Lisa smiled politely.

"How are you feeling?"

"Very well," she said in her best English pronunciation.

"Glad to hear it. Has anyone told you about Bloomsbury House?" Seeing her shake her head, he continued, "We are an organization designed to oversee children like you whom we have helped bring to England during this difficult time and if you're willing to do some work, you could actually earn some money, in addition to receiving room and board. Does that interest you?"

"Oh, yes, yes."

"Good. Now what skills do you have? What sorts of things can you do?"

"I play the piano," Lisa said proudly.

"Well, now, that's lovely, I'm sure you play beautifully, but what do you do that would be more useful? Do you sew?"

"Yes, yes, I sew."

"Good," Mr. Hardesty said, and checked a little box on the form he was filling out.

Before she knew it, she was escorted out of the office as the next child was ushered in. She was halfway down the hallway when she realized she hadn't gotten to ask about Sonia. She marched back into the office without knocking.

"I have a sister . . . in Vienna." Mr. Hardesty looked at the long line of children before him, then back to the girl with the dark red hair two feet in front of him.

"All in good time, Miss Jura," he said with a sigh, and crossed the room to escort the insistent young girl gently out of the room.

When Lisa finally arrived at Dovercourt relocation camp in Essex, three hours south of London, she was exhausted and her feet were swollen. The children's holiday camp had been hastily pressed into service to shelter the hundreds of young refugees who didn't yet have homes. She looked at all the children and again recognized no one. She supposed Mela and the other girl from the train had gone to wealthy relatives and would be sleeping in comfortable beds by now. Michael was probably prowling the streets of London looking for Sherlock Holmes.

She sat quietly and apart from the other kids in the large army-style mess hall, eating a breakfast of porridge, eggs, toast, and some strange fish called kippers. Why bother making new friends if they'd all be leaving soon anyway?

They slept on cots in drafty cabins. Lisa put on her sweater and coat and huddled under the single wool blanket against the damp December weather. She wanted to cry but was too ashamed to have the other girls hear her. Everyone was asleep. She forced herself to concentrate on the Chopin prelude that she and her mother had played together, letting her fingers float through the air over the blankets. Before she could mime the last chord, she was asleep.

The next day, she attended the makeshift English class and looked out the window as columns of cars pulled up to the main administration office. Men and women of all descriptions went in and out of the office, consulting lists and digging through the children's life histories. Groups of them would appear like specters in the back of the class, pointing to a particular child they wanted to interview. Lisa worried that her nose wasn't straight enough. That her hair was too red. She scrutinized each arrival—was this the one who would want her?

Older girls were picked first, since they could work and pay their way. Small children were chosen next by childless couples and taken to homes in the countryside. The rest waited to be sent to hostels and orphanages that were being readied by Quakers, Jewish groups, churches, and kind souls all over England. On the third day of camp, while she was participating in a gas mask training class, a hand landed on her shoulder and she was called to the office.

"Miss Jura?" began a stout English lady in sensible shoes. "We understand you like to sew, which is excellent, but we'd also like to know if you get along well with, ah, younger children."

"I have a younger sister. I'm looking for someone to help me get her out of Vienna! Can you help? Do you know anyone that—"

"First things first, my dear, let's get you settled first. There's a very important military officer who's turning his sizable mansion into a civil defense headquarters, and they need some extra help. The lady of the house has a new baby. What do you think, dear?"

Lisa was thrilled at the idea of going to a rich person's home. She'd make them love her right away and then they'd help her.

"I adore babies!"

"It's all settled, then, young lady. Someone will meet you at the station in Brighton tomorrow."

For the first time since her arrival, Lisa had hope and walked with a springy step back to the cabin. She sat on her bed, pulled out the photo of her mother, and placed it in front of her. Unfolding a sheet of paper she had torn out of her English primer, she began: "Dear Mama and Papa . . ."

She filled the letter with positive thoughts and English phrases she hoped would impress them: "I am determined not to be thought of as an *ausländer*—a foreigner—as long as I'm here, I'll try my best to be a real English girl." And then she signed it. The well-meaning but overworked camp officials hadn't thought about things like stamps, so after dinner, as the other children stacked their plates and glasses on the sideboard, Lisa walked through the double doors to the kitchen and approached a ruddy-faced dishwasher, smiling sweetly. "If I helped you wash the dishes, would you buy me a stamp for a letter?"

"Of course, young lady. There's a sponge under the sink."

Lisa grabbed a plate and started scrubbing.

6

$\mathcal{B}$RIGHTON-BY-THE-SEA was a city renowned for summer holidays and family vacations. Winter was another story.

The train station was hollow and empty and cold. Lisa was relieved to see a heavyset man in his twenties standing on the quay holding up a hand-lettered sign with her name on it. He wore a neatly pressed dark blue uniform and matching cap.

"I'm Monty," he said, offering his hand in a hearty English handshake. For a second Lisa thought he'd broken the bones in her fingers and shook them surreptitiously behind her.

He took her small suitcase and led her to an elegant black sedan. Driven to her English home by a chauffeur! If Mama could only see her now.

They drove through the brown countryside, its fallow fields neatly bordered by trees whose leafless branches stretched upward like inverted brooms. The sedan turned off the main road at a stone pillar. The sign read "Peacock Manor." At the end of a long driveway was a massive country estate house—three stories tall, with turrets decorating the left and right corners. It looked every bit like a castle from her daydreams.

Monty pulled the sedan through the elegant porte cochere and continued around to the servants entrance at the back. The cook, three maids, and a butler came out to meet her. "Welcome to Peacock Manor," said a lady with a no-nonsense air about her. "I'm Gladys, this here's Lola, and this is Betsy, and this is Carrie. And this fine man is Mr. Piedmont, our butler. You'll meet the rest of us later; come in and take a hot bath and we'll get you some tea."

As Lisa struggled to say something polite, Gladys added, "We've heard all about you, so don't you worry. We'll take good care of you."

Lisa felt conspicuous in her old wool coat, long dress, and leggings; she knew she must look shabby and that every eye was on her. She dusted herself off and tried to smile.

Gladys showed her to a small but cozy room in the servants wing and gave her a starched white maid's uniform. When she was pronounced presentable, she was ushered through the vast, ornate foyer, past a dining room with a splendid chandelier, and down a long hallway whose walls were covered with oil paintings. Lisa swung her head quickly right and left, taking in the grandeur of it all.

She was shown into the study where her sponsor, Captain Richmond, and the butler were packing oil paints, easels, and half-finished canvases into cardboard boxes. The captain was a man in his sixties and sported two patches of white hair at the edges of a pink, bald head. A fragrant pipe hung from his mouth.

"So there you are, missy." He thrust out his hand. Lisa took it, preparing for the worst, but his handshake was mercifully gentle. "Good to have you here. You make sure Gladys treats you nicely!" He winked good-naturedly at the head maid.

"Thank you," said Lisa.

"My wife looks forward to meeting you; she's off galli-vanting in Paris—back next week. Don't mind this mess. I'm giving my painting studio over to the Home Guard; we're certainly not hoping for a war, Chamberlain has my complete trust, but just in case . . . we had best be pre-pared."

Lisa was so overwhelmed that she was grateful when Gladys handed her a feather duster and led her up the large staircase into the main hall. "I can't be bothered explain-ing everything to you, so just follow along and keep your eyes open."

Lisa quickly fell into the routine of the castle. She had a keen eye for the out-of-place article and the dust that gathered in corners, and by the end of the first week Gladys seemed duly impressed.

"You might just work out," the head maid announced in front of the others at the servants dinner table.

"And coming from her tough hide, that's a huge com-pliment," laughed Monty. Gladys slapped Monty on the shoulder, and Lisa saw a sparkle in her eye. He leaned over and quickly planted a kiss on her cheek. It was a gesture that reminded her suddenly of her father and mother, and she was overwhelmed momentarily with memories; tears sprang to her eyes, so she apologized and excused herself.

That night Lisa wrote another letter to her parents. She described the elegant furnishings and grand surroundings, hoping her mother would be proud of her. She realized while writing how happy she was to be settled after weeks of uncertainty and vowed to be useful and cheerful at all times. She arose early, put on the crisp white uniform, and flipped up the starched collar in the back, trying for a more sophisticated look. By the time the sun came up, she was hard at work, scrubbing floors, fetching coal, and dusting endlessly. Often, her day was not over until well into the evening. She worked with only one purpose—to make the money her parents needed to send Sonia.

The next day she went on a tour, holding her duster aloft as an alibi. She dusted her way through bedrooms and hallways until she found what she was looking for: a piano. Any self-respecting castle like this would have one, she'd figured. It was located on the first floor, in the parlor off a guest bedroom, and was a solid baby grand. She cautiously opened the lid and ran her fingers lightly over the keys. It was out of tune, but at least the keys didn't stick, so she began a simple nocturne. Loud footsteps clattered down the hall immediately and Gladys appeared at the door, out of breath and furious.

"And what might you be doing!"

"I, I—"

"The captain's having his nap! If you wake him, there'll be hell to pay." She folded down the lid and pushed Lisa out of the room. "Now, go down to the basement and help sort through the onions. Lola needs help with the soup— and keep your hands off things that don't belong to you."

"But in Vienna, I played the piano!"

"Well, isn't that marvelous," Gladys said cuttingly.

"Yes, it is marvelous," Lisa retorted, walking down the hall and biting her tongue so as not to say: "If you only knew something about music, you'd know how marvelous it is!"

Lisa knew the captain's wife had arrived from Paris when she heard the squeal of an infant echoing through the hallways. She was introduced to the twenty-five-year-old lady of the house, who wore a cream-colored Chanel suit and matching hat. Lisa was mesmerized by her elegance. She was given the added chore of "nanny's assistant," which involved washing the baby clothes, hanging them to dry, and folding them neatly in the bassinet drawers. Unfortunately, the job also involved washing the dirty diapers or, as she soon discovered, boiling them.

One day when she was tired, she looked up at the stacks of clean diapers and told herself that no one would miss it if she tossed a dirty one in the bin. This solution was so simple that every time there was an exceptional mess, she would toss out the offending diaper. There were hundreds more waiting on the shelf.

A while later Gladys greeted her with a smelly bag. "And what, might I ask, have we here?" Monty had found her secret in the trash and fished it out. "I've counted the diapers and there's only a dozen left! You've been chucking them out, haven't you?"

"No," Lisa heard herself saying. She never lied, but she was fearful she'd be sent away. "No, I haven't." But for the rest of the day, Lisa had a terrible ache in her stomach. She was eaten up with guilt and fear and finally went to Gladys to confess. "Of course I knew you chucked 'em. I wasn't born yesterday, you know. The lady wants to see you upstairs." Lisa didn't move. "That would be now!" Gladys yelled, and Lisa ran upstairs.

She stood anxiously at the door to the grand bedroom

and imagined the worst, but the lady of the house was laughing when she opened the door. "I suppose my husband would give you a lecture about thrift—he's very proud of being thrifty. So I won't tell him about the diapers, all right?"

"Thank you, ma'am," Lisa said, and stared around the room at the clothes, the perfume bottles, and the satin-covered chairs.

"But I haven't called you in here to talk about diapers. I want you to be my lady's maid."

Lisa mouth dropped.

"My maid is pregnant and she's leaving. I'll find someone else to wash the diapers. Tomorrow she'll teach you all you need to know. Just don't throw out *my* underwear!" She laughed loudly and waved three fingers quickly in a good-bye gesture, turning back to her cosmetics table.

Every Friday Lisa was paid her salary and she stashed it proudly in a well-fingered envelope in the nightstand where she kept her mother's picture and her copy of "Clair de Lune." On Saturday, Lisa would accompany Gladys and Monty to the village for supplies. They would pile in an old pickup—Gladys and Monty in the cab and Lisa in back; occasionally she would catch them stealing a kiss. Lisa enjoyed looking out at the wide expanse of the English countryside. It was a welcome break from the routine.

One Saturday traffic came to a complete standstill. Lisa stuck her head out around the cab of the truck: The road was filled with a long green convoy of British army trucks and tanks, crawling like a centipede. She hadn't seen tanks since Hitler's army had moved into Vienna over a year ago. "Are we at war?" she asked breathlessly.

"Just getting ready in case, luv," Gladys replied, then

looked over at Monty's fascinated gaze, which followed the convoy. "Don't be getting any ideas, Monty!"

While the others shopped for groceries, Lisa wandered the high street. In the window of a secondhand shop, she saw an old red bicycle. She'd never had a bicycle; in Vienna they were important things for adults, not play toys for children. She had dreamed of the day when she would be older and could get one. She stared at the wheels— wheels that could take people to places they wanted to go someday. A honking horn disturbed her reverie, and she looked up to find Monty beckoning to her. She climbed back into the truck to return to Peacock Manor.

On special evenings, the staff cranked up the old Victrola and sang along to recordings of "Daisy, Daisy" or "Under the Spreading Chestnut Tree." The simple, melancholy tunes lingered in her head and she wished she could try them out on a piano. Sometimes she would hum "Clair de Lune" and picture the moonlight glistening off the Danube. If she closed her eyes tight enough she could picture her mother and father, with Sonia and Rosie, walking along its banks. But each time she opened her eyes Vienna would fade more and more into the distance.

Lisa thrived as the lady's maid. She carefully inspected skirts for torn hems, scoured blouses for missing buttons, and sewed in drooping shoulder pads without being asked. The lady of the house soon felt comfortable with Lisa's choices of purses to match her shoes and joked that Lisa had a better sense of style than her!

Once, Lisa got up her nerve to show the lady a new-style shoe in the fashion magazine.

"You've been stealing my magazines?" she asked with an arched eyebrow.

Lisa looked stricken.

"I'm just kidding, Lisa, you don't have to take things so seriously all the time."

But Lisa did take everything seriously. She had to. Anxious weeks went by with no return letters from her family. One day Monty handed her a beat-up blue airmail letter with a German stamp. She was overjoyed to see that the address on the letter was 13 Franzenbrückestrasse; it was postmarked a month earlier. The letter was short; her mother said simply: "Make us proud of you; we miss you every day." Monty put his arm around her when the tears came.

After dinner the staff would gather around the wireless and listen to the BBC broadcast. The news from Europe was disquieting. It had been almost a year since Hitler had annexed Austria and six months since he had taken over Sudetenland. In the three months since Lisa had been in England, she had heard nothing to ease her worry.

Lisa was tidying up the new office of the Home Guard (which had taken over the billiards room) when she heard loud voices coming from the captain's study next door.

"I told you this is what it would come to!" a man's voice shouted.

"What were we supposed to do!"

"Stop the bastard, that's what."

"It has nothing to do with us!"

When the voices quieted, Lisa could hear the frightening voice that made her shiver with fear. The voice of the Führer echoed through the manor house: *"Ein Volk, ein Reich, ein Führer!"*

She walked closer to the room where the men were gathered and stood in the hall listening, terrified by the voice of the man she so hated.

The captain was shouting. "Can you believe that madman has just marched into Czechoslovakia without a shot being fired?"

He walked into the hall, waving his arms in disgust, and caught sight of Lisa. "Aha! Come here, we need you."

He took her arm gently and led her into the room, where five uniformed men were scattered on chairs in front of the radio.

"What is this maniac saying now?" he asked.

"*Ausrottung, es ist nichts unmöglich!*" came the bone-chilling voice of Hitler.

"Extermination . . . nothing is impossible," Lisa translated slowly, growing more upset with each word.

An officer, seeing her distress, exclaimed: "Have a heart, don't make the poor girl listen to this."

"All right, dear, that's enough. Thank you," the Captain said.

A young girl shouldn't hear it? Lisa asked herself. I have lived it, I have seen it! She thought of Kristallnacht and saw her father on the ground, naked and humiliated, an image she could not erase from her mind. Suddenly, she was overwhelmed with a desire to be with others like her. Yes, Monty was friendly, Gladys meant well, and the lady was kind, too; she had enough to eat and she was safe; it should be enough, she told herself, but it wasn't.

It was hard to get back to the routine of her job, but Lisa dutifully laid out the mistress's outfits and matched the shoes to the purse and the skirt to the jacket. As always, the lady was very pleased.

"A wonderful choice, Lisa."

"Thank you, ma'am," Lisa said. Her heart had been heavy with guilt. She needed to ask the most important question, and she'd been putting it off. "Madam? May I ask you something?"

"Certainly, what is it?"

"I have a sister in Vienna. She's very sweet and she could work in the kitchen. We very much need someone to sponsor her so she can get on the kinder train, and if there's any—"

The lady looked at her, interrupting. "How old is she?"

"Twelve."

The lady frowned.

"She'll be thirteen in a week," Lisa added, exaggerating. "I'd take care of her on my time off. She'd be no trouble, I promise. She's very well behaved. . . ."

The lady gave her a sad smile. "I wish I could make these kinds of decisions on my own . . . but I promise I'll ask my husband. You've got nerve, I like that."

Sunday morning came and Gladys came into Lisa's room as usual. "Are you certain I can't coax you to church? There's a lot of young boys there! Might be fun. It'd get you out of the house."

"No, thank you," Lisa said politely. She couldn't imagine the idea of going to church. She listened to Gladys and Monty's laughter echo through the hall, as they made their way out the kitchen door and into the pickup. She lay on her bed and listened to the wind rustling through the leaves out the window.

She missed her family so. Closing her eyes she pictured the ceramic tailor of Dresden on the sideboard of the living room and scanned the pictures on the wall in her mind's eye. This was her ritual; she was determined not to forget a thing. She imagined she could hear her parents speaking in their native German—and missed their voices.

The wind reminded her of the last movement of the Chopin Sonata in B Minor. She got up and crept to the distant room where the piano was. She sat on the bench, lifted the lid, and put her fingers to the keys. Everyone was away, but still she was frightened—so she played the keys with silent strokes, not making a sound. Her fingers flew over the familiar patterns and for a moment she felt a great joy, connected to her music and to her family, even if it was only in her imagination. This was what her mother had begged her to do, so she played for her mother, and she played for herself, for the joy of it, until she could hear the sounds of the footsteps returning. Then she crept secretly back to her room.

The next day Lisa was polishing the two-toned open-toed pumps in the walk-in closet off the lady's bedroom. The lady had seemed upset about many things—about the baby's colic, about the Home Guard officers' cigar smoke, about the perfume she had spilled—about the day in general. She called Lisa into the boudoir, where she was seated at the mirror.

"I've talked to the captain," she said. "Unfortunately we won't be able to take on another person . . . I'm sorry."

The words fell heavily on Lisa and seemed to fall heavily on the lady as well. "You see, he's given half the house to the government and he feels he's done his duty."

"Thank you for asking him," Lisa said softly.

The woman kept powdering her face, and Lisa turned to go.

"Lisa? How old are you?"

"I'll be fifteen."

"That's a wonderful age. I wish I were fifteen again."
The woman's voice was distant, unhappy. Lisa didn't know
how to respond. "When I was fifteen, I thought the world
was my oyster. I thought I was going to make something of
my life. . . ." She looked directly into Lisa's eyes. "I'm
sorry. . . ."

The lady's voice trailed off. "Lay out my green jacket,
would you?"

"Make something of yourself." The phrase ran through
Lisa's mind as she ironed the jackets, pressed the skirts,
and polished the shoes. Over and over came the calm
voice of her mother—its gentle insistence invading her
thoughts. Whom could she look to for guidance if not her
mother?

That night she slept fitfully, tossing and turning as the
summer rains beat down on the slanted roof close to her
head. In the morning, she was awakened by a rap at the
door.

"Are you coming or not, sleepyhead?" Gladys yelled.

She dressed hurriedly, opened the drawer, and grabbed
the envelope that held the money she had saved from her
wages, stuffing it into her pocket.

The weekly trip to town didn't have the same carefree
air it normally did. Gladys and Monty seemed sad, sitting
close to one another but saying nothing. Was it a lovers'
quarrel? Lisa had never had a boyfriend, and it seemed so
mysterious. She watched Gladys lean her head on Monty's
huge shoulder; there were tears in her eyes.

Lisa helped Gladys pick through the parsnips and celery
while Monty headed for the high street with a purposeful
stride.

"You're watching the last steps of a free man," the head

maid said, watching him go. "The big lout is signing up for the navy today."

"The navy?" Lisa asked, filled with wonder.

"There's a rumor that the mobilization is going to be announced any minute; he wanted to beat them to it."

Lisa, filled with emotion, kept staring at Monty.

In an uncharacteristic gesture, Gladys put her arm around Lisa. "He'll show those Germans, you'll see . . . it's going to be all right." But Gladys started to cry. "I'm sorry, luv, look at this silly blubbering."

They finished the shopping and Lisa carried the heavy vegetables to the truck.

"May I do an errand, ma'am?"

"Go ahead, of course you can."

Lisa doubled back around the corner and found the secondhand shop. She summoned up all her courage and walked in.

"I want to buy the bicycle," she said, trying as hard as she could to pronounce the "w" the way the English people did. She saw the curious expression of the shopkeeper and knew her accent was still dreadfully foreign.

"So, you must be that refugee we've heard about. My wife told me we had one of you nearby."

"Yes," Lisa said, feeling self-conscious.

"And you're looking for a bicycle?"

"Yes . . . I have money."

The man walked up to the bike that Lisa was pointing to and looked at the tag. "Four pound two shillings. Hmm, seems a bit pricey for what it is. How does two pound sound?" he asked with a wink.

Lisa fished in her envelope and handed two large coins to the man. She fought back a feeling of guilt; this was the money for Sonia! But she'd make more money soon, she promised herself.

"Can you keep it here until I come to get it?"

"Whenever you need it, it'll be here."

7

$\mathscr{L}$ISA WAITED until the day after she was paid her small wages, then arose before dawn and packed her things. The sun was coming up when she tiptoed into the kitchen and opened the cupboard. She cut a wedge of cheese from under the damp towel in the larder and took bite after bite, fearful of the hunger that had so often gnawed at her during the last months in Vienna. She cut a portion of dried meat, wrapped it in newspaper, and stuffed it in her coat pocket.

The cold damp of dawn greeted her as she opened the back door. She stood on the threshold for a long moment, then came back into the warmth of the kitchen, drawn by the kindness she had felt in this house. Using the pencil Gladys kept for the grocery list, she wrote carefully: "Thank you. I'm sorry, Lisa Jura."

She walked the two miles to the village. When the secondhand shop opened, she collected her red bike, tied her small suitcase to the back, and was off. The sun was just breaking through the morning fog as she left the village. The sign read: "Brighton—45 miles."

The rhythm of the pedals reminded her of a toccata and fugue by Bach, which she began to hum as she flew through the countryside, passing cows in the fields and birds on the telephone wires. She tapped out its staccato beat with her feet and began to sing at full volume. She was happy; she was free! She was going to London. She would go to Bloomsbury House and make them find a place for her in the big city.

As the day wore on and the miles got longer, she was hit by a wave of indecision. Was it terrible to have left a house with caring people who fed and sheltered her? The captain's wife must hate her now; Gladys and Monty must think the worst of refugees. Would she even make it to London?

But she kept pedaling and began to chant aloud: "I will go to London. I will go to London." With sheer force of will, and with every yard of distance between her and the castle, she left her indecision behind.

She waited to eat as long as she could, then pulled over to the side of the road, leaned her bike against a hedge, and pulled out the precious piece of meat she'd taken from the pantry. She nibbled carefully, determined to keep some for later. The countryside was quiet, and the bees were at work in the hayfields. The tall grass soothed her aching legs. In no time she was asleep, dreaming of Franzenbrückestrasse. People were running down the streets, and her mother was yelling, "Find Papa, find Papa!" She was running through piles and piles of broken glass, looking for her father. The piles of glass got deeper and deeper and felt sharper under her feet.

She jerked awake and was frightened to see a figure

hunched over her—a face right next to hers, a cold hand on her thigh. She screamed and scrambled to her feet, throwing the man to the side.

"Wait a second, good-looking; don't run off so fast!" The man was middle-aged and ill shaven and looked as if he'd been working in the fields. He moved to Lisa's bike and put both hands on the handlebars ominously.

"Don't be running anywhere just yet."

Lisa's heart was beating furiously. "Give me my bike."

But the man stood still, smiling menacingly. She stepped quickly into the middle of the road, looking frantically up and down, but it was completely deserted. When she looked back, she saw the man wheeling her bike behind the hedge.

"Let me show you something, good-looking," he said, wheeling the bike farther and farther away from the road.

Lisa forced herself to keep her wits about her. She considered running away, but everything she had in the world was in the suitcase strapped to the bike. She had to stall until a car came down the road.

"Wait! I can't walk, I've hurt my foot," she said, throwing herself back to the ground near the edge of the road. "I think I have broken my foot."

The man looked at her skeptically but wheeled the bike back to where she sat on the ground.

"Come talk to me," Lisa said, smiling flirtatiously. "Do you work near here?" The man nodded and came over, leaning against the hedge. He brought out a hand-rolled cigarette and lit it.

"I work very near here," Lisa pressed on. "Perhaps I could meet you later."

Every minute that went by was an eternity but she hid her terror and made false promise after false promise about a fictitious rendezvous. Luckily, the man was gullible and arrogant, nodding his head and smiling. Finally, ten agonizing minutes later, she heard the noise of a vehicle in the distance.

As it approached, she jumped up and lurched into the road, waving her arms frantically. A military jeep pulled to a stop in front of her.

"Sorry, miss, no riders, government orders."

Before Lisa could even explain about her attacker, the man had fled into the field and disappeared. Trembling, she thanked the soldier, got on her bike and pedaled as fast and as far as she could.

She entered the outskirts of the city of Brighton at nightfall and followed the signs to the train station. Her muscles were shaking as she got off the bike and limped up to the ticket master's booth.

"The next train to London?" she asked wearily.

"Not till morning, six-eighteen, track four."

She fished for the required shillings and pence from her pocket, and was handed a ticket.

"Is that your bicycle?"

Lisa nodded.

"You'll have to wait for the afternoon train, then; no bikes allowed on the commuter express."

"Are you sure?"

"Rules are rules."

Lisa hung her head and wheeled her bicycle through the station, finally finding the ladies' room, grateful to see a small wooden bench inside. She lay down on it and put her head on her suitcase. She was too tired to dream.

The sound of the flushing toilet woke her up. Two giggling teenage girls in school uniforms were putting on lipstick and laughing, oblivious of Lisa's presence. "Hurry up!" one of them yelled to the other. "You'll miss the train."

Lisa hurried, too, grabbing her things and running onto the platform. The train doors were open and inviting. She glanced back at her red bicycle, said good-bye, and boarded.

The compartment was crowded, but she found a seat next to a group of teenage boys with green duffel bags. She supposed they were being called up for the draft as part of the national mobilization. Their faces were soft and young; one of them was covered in pimples. She didn't think they stood a chance against the steely-eyed Nazi soldiers she had seen at home, and a dark mood of worry seized her. Lisa tried to distract herself by looking out the window at the lush green countryside, steering her mind onto a more cheerful path of thoughts about the big city ahead of her.

Waterloo station was filled to the brim with travelers. Whole families were on the move, and porters were wheeling huge carts overflowing with suitcases. The warm smell from a bakery stall made her stomach ache, and she went and ordered a hot-cross bun. She made herself eat slowly so she could enjoy it; it seemed like the most delicious bun on earth.

Following the careful directions of helpful pedestrians, Lisa walked the weary miles to Bloomsbury House.

8

$\mathcal{T}$HE BLOOMSBURY HOUSE was still a madhouse of volunteers, arriving children, and file boxes. Lisa walked down the hall in guilty trepidation and gave her name to one of the secretaries.

"Have a seat, dearie, he'll be with you soon as he's able. Care for some tea?"

She accepted gratefully and watched as boxes of donations were sorted and stacked. Britain had responded to the arrival of the Kindertransports with an outpouring of cutlery, linens, rocking horses, and dolls; all manner of whatnots seemed to have landed in the hallway in front of her. The offices were full; the overflow of prospective foster parents spilled into corners and onto stairwells.

"I know you said you could only take two, but it would be terrible to break up the family," a volunteer implored into a telephone. "They're so lovely, and very well behaved, too." The worker glanced at the three children next to her who were holding tight to one another's hands.

Her eyes were sparkling in encouragement, and her chin nodded up and down.

Lisa wondered how she'd be described—not well behaved certainly, more like a troublemaker. No matter, she'd made her decision. She wouldn't go back. Anything, she told herself, was better than the terrible loneliness of the last six months.

The volunteers continued their phone calling and their cajoling, fielding offers of buildings to be converted to orphanages and giving advice on bedwetting and tantrums. Lisa accepted more and more cookies.

"Lisa Jura? Mr. Hardesty will see you now." She walked into his office and half imagined that Mr. Hardesty groaned when he saw the dark red hair approach.

"Aha, it's you!" he said as recognition dawned. "We were worried—the captain told us you'd gone missing." But instead of the brash young bundle of energy he remembered, before him stood an exhausted girl with uncombed hair and wrinkled clothes. Lisa was too tired to think of anything to say.

Mr. Hardesty picked up a file with Lisa's picture on the front and several papers clipped to the back.

"Were they treating you badly?"

Lisa reddened in embarrassment. "No, sir."

"Were you getting enough to eat?"

"Yes, sir."

Mr. Hardesty let out a large breath, exhaling weeks and months of fatigue and frustration. He loosened his collar. He was sweltering in the airless August afternoon.

Lisa forced herself to begin the speech she had rehearsed over and over in her head. "I want to make something of myself. I don't want to be a servant. I want to learn something. Please, let me stay in London."

Mr. Hardesty studied this outspoken young woman and let out another long breath. "I'm afraid that's very difficult. So many people are leaving London, and I don't know if I could find a family here to take you. The hostels are full up."

"People are leaving?" Lisa said, her eyes filled with fear.

Mr. Hardesty softened his expression. "Didn't you get any news down there? Most people are expecting a war—and I'm afraid I am, too. Looks like Warsaw will be next. Chamberlain is over there now pleading, but it won't come to anything, if you want my opinion."

He looked at her proud but vulnerable expression and added, "We'd prefer to send as many of you to the countryside as we can. Most people expect we'll be bombed."

"Please, don't send me back. I can work in a factory! I need to make some money to send to my parents to bring Sonia over."

"Sonia?" Mr. Hardesty asked.

"My sister, Sonia. I'm hoping she will come soon on the Kindertransport."

"What's her name, again?"

"Sonia Jura, from Vienna."

"He fumbled for a long time through a file box and finally located a typed card. "Sonia Jura, aha. Yes, but we don't have a sponsor for her yet. If she doesn't have a sponsor, they won't let her into England."

"What if they don't find one?" Lisa pressed.

"We are doing our best, but it's very difficult right now, there are so many who need sponsors."

"Please let me stay in London, I'll help look for someone, too, I promise," she begged.

Mr. Hardesty sighed. "Let me see what I can do, at least temporarily."

He ran his index finger down a list of telephone numbers wedged under the glass top of his desk, picked up the phone, and dialed.

"I'll get a tongue-lashing, but hopefully it'll be a short one," he muttered.

Lisa watched as Mr. Hardesty wrinkled up his face and began: "Mrs. Cohen? Alfred Hardesty, here, Bloomsbury House. We have a bit of an unusual situation here, and I know I promised not to send so much as one more sardine your way, but there's a lovely young lady just needs a place for a month. . . ."

He held the phone away from his ear and Lisa heard the raised voice of a woman. Cupping his hand over the mouthpiece, Mr. Hardesty leaned forward and said sotto voce: "I think you two will get along famously."

Anxious to get some relief from the heat, and concerned about smoothing Mrs. Cohen's ruffled feathers, Mr. Hardesty himself escorted Lisa to her new home: the hostel at 243 Willesden Lane, in Willesden Green, a twenty-minute taxi ride from the Bloomsbury House. Willesden Green was an older neighborhood of large brick houses. Its corners were alive with tiny shops—a butcher's, a druggist's, a laundry, and a bakery. Only one shop was boarded and had a sign: "Long Live Britain, God Bless You All."

The houses on Willesden Lane were surrounded by neatly manicured lawns. As the taxi slowed, Lisa noticed a building with a cross carved into the stone lintel above the door; three nuns were in the front flower garden, watering the plants. The cab rolled to a stop at the next house, a rambling three-story structure whose shutters and fence were in need of paint, but whose lawn was recently mowed and trimmed. Its semicircular driveway was bordered with a fringe of lilacs.

The two of them got out and headed up the stone walkway. Mr. Hardesty knocked and, while waiting, adjusted the crooked bronze numbers 2-4-3 back into alignment.

An imposing middle-aged woman in a dark purple dress opened the door. She had a rigid, upper-class bearing and held her chin tilted upward. It looked to Lisa as though she were trying to balance the huge, tightly wound bun of auburn hair so it wouldn't fall off the top of her head.

"Please come in." She surveyed Lisa and glanced at the little suitcase. "Is that all you have?"

"Yes, ma'am."

"Come in then! Let's not stand here while the house fills up with flies."

Mr. Hardesty picked up Lisa's suitcase and put his arm around her shoulder, easing her through the doorway.

Lisa walked into a dark-paneled foyer, which opened into a pleasant drawing room with two sofas and several groups of chairs and tables. Two well-worn chess boards were arranged neatly on top of a card table. A graceful staircase led upstairs, and a dining room was visible across the foyer. She stepped farther into the parlor and saw the large fireplace and the bay window that looked out on the convent next door. Nestled in the cove by the window was a distinctive shape, covered with a hand-crocheted shawl.

Lisa's heart beat faster; it was a piano!

"We're overcrowded, you know. We can only make room for you temporarily," Mrs. Cohen said, not noticing Lisa's expression of wonder. "I'll have one of the girls tell you the rules."

Mrs. Cohen's firm stride took her to the base of the

stairs. "Gina Kampf, come down here, please!" she shouted in a remarkably strong voice.

She has an even heavier German accent than I do, Lisa thought to herself, smiling. She felt comfortable here already.

At the sound of youthful steps thundering down the staircase, Mrs. Cohen turned to Mr. Hardesty. "While you're here, Alfred, I have some receipts I'd like to go over with you."

Mr. Hardesty turned to Lisa and shook her hand. "Now, please mind Mrs. Cohen; she has her hands full with all of you and I don't want to hear any stories about any more, ah, unexpected trips, all right?" Lisa knew he thought her a troublemaker, but she'd show him. She would make something of herself, and then he'd understand.

"Hi, I'm Gina!" A pretty, dark-haired girl with vivacious eyes finished bounding down the stairs. "You must be the new girl."

"Yes, I'm Lisa Jura."

"Pleased to meet you!" she said with an exaggerated bow. "Isn't my English fabulous? Mrs. Cohen says I'm the best English speaker in the whole house. Oh, that's the first rule, she says you have to speak English on the first floor at all times. There are millions of rules, but don't worry, I'll go over everything."

Gina started running back up the stairs. "Come on, hurry up! I'll show you our room, you'll be in with me and Ruth and Edith and Ingrid. I'm so glad you're here; Edith and Ingrid are really boring."

Lisa was shown a bedroom with two bunk beds and a small army cot wedged against the wall. There was hardly room to walk. Gina pulled open a large drawer and pushed some clothes to the side.

"Here, you can share this drawer with Edith, she won't mind."

The beds were neatly made, and nothing in the room was out of place.

"Where is everyone?" Lisa asked.

"Everybody's working! We all have jobs. You'll have to get one, too, you know. I'm only here because I help Mrs. Cohen do the books on Fridays—because my English is so good. The matron speaks dreadfully, but she doesn't care, she's old and doesn't need to impress anybody."

Lisa put down the suitcase and went to the window. She surveyed the large lawn where two ten-year-old boys were playing soccer. "That's Arnold and Shepsel. They're too young to work, so they get to play all day, the creeps," explained her exuberant roommate.

Gina headed out the door. "Come on, come on! I'll show you the washroom. There's only one for all seventeen girls, and we're not allowed to use the boys' upstairs unless we're dying or something." Lisa looked at the small bathroom with its gleaming white bathtub and tried to conjure up the image of seventeen girls fighting for a place in front of the mirror.

The tour continued. She was shown the third floor where the boys slept, met the cook, a blond Czechoslovakian named Mrs. Glazer, and was told too many rules to remember. Curfew was ten, lights out ten-thirty, no food allowed in the bedrooms (for fear of mice), hot bath once a week (to save coal), telephone calls no longer than one minute (egg timer on the table), chores on Saturday, obligatory picnic Sundays (to boost morale).

Gina kept chattering and laughing and gossiping about

everything and everyone. Lisa tried to follow it all, but she could hardly keep her eyes open. She heard herself offer a weak thank-you and fell onto the cot for a nap. She'd had a difficult twenty-four hours.

When she awoke, the house was transformed by the commotion of thirty-two children. German and Yiddish and Czech and English mixed together in the hall. The smell of roasting meat drifted into the room while the sounds of loud footsteps mixed with the screeching of chairs and tables from downstairs.

"Hurry up! You're late, I let you nap as long as I could!" Gina said. "Mrs. Cohen will have our heads if we're late for *Shabbes*."

Shabbes! Lisa had forgotten it was Friday. *Shabbes!* It had been six months without it. She looked out the window and saw that the sun was setting. Jumping up, she combed her hair, smoothed her skirt the best she could, and ran downstairs.

The thirty-two children ranged in age from ten to seventeen and sat at two long tables in the dining room. Chairs and stools of varying heights had been pressed into service. The ones on stools couldn't fit their legs under the table. The room was so tightly packed that some of the children had to crawl under the table to reach the chairs on the other side. Gina had graciously saved the seat next to her for Lisa, who was the last to arrive. She felt like she was sitting down to dinner at a carnival merry-go-round. A hush fell over the room and all eyes turned to Mrs. Cohen, who made a gesture to Mrs. Glazer.

The cook then lit the two candles and moved her arms in the circular gesture of the *berachah*, saying, "Blessed art

Thou, King of the Universe, Who commands us to kindle the Sabbath candles."

Lisa recited the prayer along with the others, feeling like crying because of the deep feeling it evoked in her. It was the first time someone other than her mother had lit the candles, and she ached for her presence.

Then the challah bread was blessed and passed around the table; each child broke off a piece and ate.

It was Mrs. Glazer again who began the prayer over the wine. Gina leaned over and whispered conspiratorially to Lisa. "Mrs. Glazer has to do it because Mrs. Cohen doesn't know the words. Somebody said she doesn't like to admit she's Jewish!"

When the prayers were over, the children attacked the platters of food, spooning the chicken and dumplings and string beans onto their plates. The girls assigned to kitchen duty got up from the table to ferry additional items to and from the kitchen.

Partway through the meal, Mrs. Cohen tapped her fork against her water glass and cleared her throat. "We have a new girl tonight, Lisa Jura. She is from Vienna. I want all of you to take the time after dinner to introduce yourselves to her courteously."

The instant Mrs. Cohen stopped speaking, the children resumed eating, hardly missing a beat. Lisa was momentarily hurt by the lack of interest, but Gina leaned over to explain. "There's always somebody coming or going—after dinner I'll introduce you to the interesting people, don't worry."

The children ate as rapidly as possible, knowing that the special food of *Shabbes* disappeared more quickly than the ordinary fare. The faster one ate, the more food one got.

Mrs. Cohen tried to preserve some dignity by slowing down the worst offenders. "Nathan? Put your fork down and count to twenty. Let someone else have a dumpling, would you?"

When the food was gone, Mrs. Cohen again tapped her fork on her wineglass. "Does anyone have any news they would like to share?"

Everyone quieted down.

"I understand you received a letter today, Paul," she continued, turning to a blond sixteen-year-old with wavy hair. "Is it something you'd like to talk about?"

Paul felt all eyes turn his way; he wiped his mouth neatly and folded his napkin. "My parents have written to say they are no longer in Berlin. Their apartment has been taken away."

The others listened carefully to Paul as he said the difficult words. "They have gone to live with people they know in Munich, but they aren't sure they'll be able to stay there long. They are looking for visas to Shanghai; I hope my brother will be coming soon on the train."

As they all listened, each child thought of his own parent, his own nightmare, his own hope.

Lisa thought of her parents and wondered if they would be able to stay in their apartment. She looked around the table at the others and saw her own sadness mirrored in their faces. They shared a terrible anxiety. It was odd, she thought, how being with others like herself made her fears easier to endure. Part of the weight of the great loneliness she had felt since her arrival in England was lifting. Now, maybe, she could almost bear the long wait until she could see her mother and father again.

*   *   *

After dinner, the younger boys raced to the living room and took dibs on who would be first at the game boards. Two dark-haired boys sat down at the chess set and resumed their game. Several of the girls pulled out their knitting bags; soon there was a clacking of needles. Because it was the Sabbath, the large wooden radio set in the corner was silent.

Gina took Lisa's arm and sat her next to her on the sofa, determined to be the arbiter of all news about "who was who."

"See the boys playing chess? The one facing us is Gunter. He's got a crush on me, but I'm still deciding. The other one is a dreamboat, but he has a girlfriend, the rat. Oh, by the way, whatever you do, don't disturb Mrs. Cohen after dinner. See that door?"

Lisa turned around and saw a closed door at the end of the downstairs hallway.

"That's her room. People say she's got gold and jewels stashed inside. I don't think anyone's ever been there, though."

The front door opened and a sixteen-year-old with a leather jacket walked in with a swagger. Lisa's eyes widened at his handsome arrogance. Gina waved at him.

"Aaron, come here a minute, meet the new girl," said Gina. "This is Lisa."

"Hi, I'm Aaron," the boy replied easily, with a bright white smile.

"Hi," she said, fascinated by the unshaven stubble on his chin.

"I hope you don't believe anything Gina's telling you, I'm sure none of it's true," he joked.

"Aaron! What a mean thing to say!" Gina said with every ounce of charm she possessed.

"Just kidding," he said, winking, then headed for the kitchen.

"Why is he here so late?" Lisa asked, curious to find out more about him.

"He's the mystery man, isn't that fabulous?"

The rest of the evening brought a parade of nice faces saying polite words to Lisa. Only one person didn't come forward, a very large boy who had spent the evening writing in a notebook. He was more than six feet tall, and his forearms and biceps were gigantic.

"Who's that?" Lisa asked.

"That's Johnny, otherwise known as Johnny 'King Kong,' Gina said, snickering.

"Johnny what?" Lisa asked.

"Didn't you see the movie *King Kong?* King Kong is a big ape just like him!"

"That's not very nice," Lisa said.

"It's just a nickname, silly."

But Lisa still thought it was an insult and resolved to be nice to the hulking boy with the serious face. "What's he writing?"

"How would I know? He doesn't show it to anybody," Gina answered.

At ten-thirty it was lights out. Putting her head on the pillow, Lisa heard wave after wave of polite nice-to-meet-yous drifting through her brain and realized she couldn't remember anybody's name.

Gina was still gossiping when Lisa fell asleep on the bed next to her.

9

$\mathcal{G}$INA TOLD Lisa that she was sure the garment factory in the East End, where she worked, needed more girls on the assembly line. Almost all the children of 243 Willesden Lane had jobs; and three-quarters of the salaries of each went to the hostel coffers for room and board.

Lisa begged Gina to go by bus—the huge double-decker red bus that fascinated her so. What she didn't say was that the idea of the underground train she'd heard about terrified her—and she didn't want Gina to think she was a scaredy-cat. The two new friends walked down Willesden Lane, past Paddington Cemetery to Kilburn High Street where a dozen people were queuing up neatly. The bus rumbled up several minutes later and they got on, running up the spiral staircase to the top deck.

The second-story view was divine. Lisa looked out excitedly as they sped down Edgeware Road to the Marble Arch, where the magnificent expanse of Hyde Park began. Elegant women were pushing wicker prams, and obedient pugs, corgis, and spaniels were held tight by their leashes. London was mercifully crowded and civilized, a welcome change from the slow pace of the countryside near Brighton.

Gina shared some of her early adventures with Lisa. She, too, had been assigned a servant's job when she first arrived, in a large family home in Sussex, and she, too, had found a way to leave.

The other fact that bonded them was that they were both from Vienna.

"Didn't you love the opera house? Isn't it the most beautiful place in the world?" Gina asked.

"Yes, oh, yes," Lisa fibbed. She had never been inside the Vienna Grand Court Opera House she had so admired from a distance. Only rich people could afford the opera, and Lisa soon realized from her new friend's descriptions of fur coats and oil paintings, silver and servants, that Gina's family background was worlds removed from her own on Franzenbrückestrasse.

The two girls, however, shared the same worry about the fate of their parents. Gina spoke about the letters from her parents and how they had been forced to wear yellow stars and carry identification cards with the large letter J. Lisa was aghast.

She stared into the street below, taking in the recruitment posters for the RAF and the piles of sandbags; she realized that Britain was also worried about Hitler. First Austria, then Sudetenland, then Czechoslovakia; who would be next? Would the Nazis come here? The huge block letters of the poster advertising the *Evening Standard* spelled the day's headline: POLAND TREMBLES.

"Look! Look! That's where the king and queen live," Gina yelled over the noise of the bus. They had turned left and were passing the gold-tipped metal gates in front of Buckingham Palace.

Lisa strained to get a glimpse of royalty but could see no one but the palace guards in their huge bearskin helmets.

"The princess is the same age as I am," Gina said proudly.

"Who's the princess?" Lisa asked, hating to sound so naive.

"Princess Elizabeth! She's fifteen!"

How thrilling to be so close to something so exciting, so royal. Lisa was beginning to like this England. And I'm the same age as the Princess, too, she thought.

The bus wove through the crowded financial district and crossed the Thames River at Tower Bridge. Before them lay the docks and warehouses; huge cranes lined the river, loading waiting barges with all manner of crates and machinery.

The garment factory was in the predominantly Jewish part of the Cockney East End and was a three-story brick building with folding warehouse doors that read "Platz & Sons" in faded letters. Inside were long rows of sewing machines, with scores of women in scarves bent over them, making a deafening racket. The air was stale and filled with dust.

Seeing her friend's startled expression, Gina laughed: "You'll get used to it," and brought Lisa over to meet the foreman, Mr. Dimble. She kissed her friend good-bye and went to work.

Mr. Dimble motioned for her to follow him into a crowded office. "Ever use a sewing machine before?" he asked quickly, sparing the niceties.

"Yes, my father is a tailor."

"Let's get a little taste of it, then," he said, and ushered her back onto the floor. "Mabel, stand up for a second, would you kindly?"

A woman in her forties with thick glasses stood up. Mr. Dimble picked up two pieces of navy blue cloth from the floor, placed them together, and handed the fabric to Lisa.

"Let's give it a try."

Lisa sat confidently at the machine, lifted the presser foot, inserted the two pieces of cloth, and pushed the foot pedal. She produced a perfectly straight seam.

"You're hired," Mr. Dimble said. "Come back tomorrow morning—eight-thirty—and we'll set you up. Come to the office and I'll go over your papers."

Lisa handed him her alien registration book, which he stamped and handed back.

Thanking him profusely, she left and looked for Gina down the line of machines, but bolts of cloth and mannequins blocked her view. She waved anyway, and several nice ladies waved back.

The foreman had explained that the best way back to London northwest was by the underground and that the station was just a block away. Buoyed by the optimism her employment had brought her, she decided to give it a go. How scary could it be?

The station at Whitechapel was marked by a large sign: "London Underground." She melded into the stream of people passing through the turnstiles, and before she knew it she was stepping onto a large wooden escalator going down, down, down. The tubular passageway was enormous and deep.

Lisa couldn't imagine how they had ever dug such a hole. At the end of the escalator, the people flowed down a white tile corridor and spilled onto a platform. A train burst through the black opening and screeched to a stop. She stepped across the gap, landing safely aboard the train, and was very proud of herself indeed.

She followed her instructions to Willesden Green station, got off without a hitch, and headed up Walm Lane. On the corner was a shop with the enticing odor of fish and chips, and Lisa watched a large man in work boots through the window as he sprinkled vinegar on the treasure in front of him. She was starving but only had a tuppence in her pocket. Perhaps Mrs. Glazer had a pot of something stewing on the stove.

Continuing up the street, she saw a woman working in the front garden of a nondescript brick house. The middle-aged lady wore a plain black dress, and her white hair was pulled severely back in a bun.

The woman stared intensely at Lisa as she walked by; the effect was chilling, but she remembered how her mother had told her to be friendly to one's neighbors. Despite her hunger and exhaustion, she did what the voice inside told her to do.

"Good afternoon! I'm a new neighbor from up the block," Lisa said.

The scary woman gave a curt nod, then turned back to her vegetables. Lisa shivered and walked on.

The door to the hostel was kept locked from 9 to 4:30 when most of the children were at work. Lisa rang the bell and Mrs. Glazer let her in.

"Any luck?" the cook asked in a friendly tone.

"Yes, I start tomorrow," Lisa replied, and trying not to sound too desperate, she added, "Is there any lunch left?"

"Of course, we'll find you something."

Lisa rested on her bed after eating and enjoyed the eerie quiet of the hostel. Mrs. Cohen was out shopping, and the two youngsters were at the synagogue nearby, learning Hebrew.

She pictured the living room downstairs and the treasure it held. It was now or never, she thought. She got up, went downstairs, and walked to the piano, gently pulling back the shawl that covered it.

Looking around guiltily, she lifted the lid covering the keys. A Bechstein—the professor had told her they were very good pianos. She sat down and stretched her fingers silently over the keys. It had been almost nine months since she had played a piano; would her fingers work at all?

Slowly, she began the opening theme of the Grieg Piano Concerto in A Minor. With a shiver of delight, she attacked the keyboard in earnest.

She felt a strange sensation—as if someone else were playing and she were only a spectator. She was oblivious to everything. She didn't notice out the window that the nun had stopped watering the hyacinths next door or that Mrs. Glazer had come out of the kitchen and was peeking in from the foyer.

Finally, during a soft, lyrical passage, Lisa's reverie was interrupted by footsteps. She turned to see Paul, the blond boy, trying to shut the front door quietly so she wouldn't be disturbed.

"Please don't stop, it sounds so lovely," he said, smiling.

Lisa played on as one by one the children arrived home. Even before they could open the door they heard the music, hypnotic and beautiful. Without saying a word, they gathered in the living room, on the stairs—anywhere they could hear.

Edith slithered to the sideboard, took out her knitting, and settled in for the concert.

Somewhere into the third, thunderous movement, Mrs.

Cohen came through the door carrying a box of groceries; she stopped and stared. Lisa saw her and immediately stopped playing.

"Listen to Lisa!" Edith said proudly to Mrs. Cohen. "She can play the piano!"

Mrs. Cohen responded with a slight nod and continued on toward the back of the house.

"Don't stop!" Edith begged Lisa.

"Oh, play something else, please!" asked Gunter, coming over to stand by her side.

Lisa began Beethoven's 32 Variations in C Minor; she hoped she would remember the notes. Paul came closer, too, and watched in wonder as her nimble fingers flew over the keys.

Thrilled by the attention, Lisa launched into her favorite, "Clair de Lune," just as Gina came in the door, followed closely by Aaron. When Gina saw her friend at the piano, surrounded by all the boys, she couldn't believe her eyes.

"Gina, come listen!" Gunter said.

In spite of her immediate jealousy, Gina came over and stood transfixed by the music.

"You sound just like Myra Hess," Aaron said, reverently.

"You've heard about Myra Hess?" Lisa said, her eyes shining at the handsome boy.

"Who is Myra Hess?" Gina said, dying to be included.

"A famous pianist, silly."

"Well, pardon me!" Gina said.

"I've seen her at the Royal Albert Hall," Aaron boasted.

"No, you haven't!" Paul and Gunter said in unison.

"Maybe I have, maybe I haven't, maybe I'll get tickets next time she plays," Aaron said charmingly.

Lisa continued playing the Debussy. The room grew hushed, everyone transfixed by the beauty of the music.

Lisa was the star of dinner; she hardly got to touch her food. Everyone wanted to know where she had learned to play so well and how long she had studied. Gina sat at the other end of the table talking with Edith, unhappy to see her popularity usurped but putting on a good face. Mrs. Cohen watched silently from the head of the table.

After the meal, the matron switched on the large wooden radio in the living room and everyone gathered to listen to the BBC. A reporter was giving details of a British negotiating team, which was headed for Russia, where they would try to make an agreement with the Soviets to block Hitler's expected advance into Poland. It was August of 1939.

When the broadcast was over, the children resumed their chess games and conversations. As the din of the evening's social hour got under way, Mrs. Cohen said in her formal voice: "Lisa, would you please follow me to my room."

Everyone looked up in surprise. Gina looked at Lisa with an expression that said she feared the worst. Lisa followed the large woman to her room in trepidation.

"I see you've studied the piano," Mrs. Cohen said, closing the door behind her.

"Yes, ma'am," Lisa answered, taking in Mrs. Cohen's small room. It had an old world warmth that reminded her of her parents' bedroom in Vienna; there was a four-poster bed with a thick duvet, and next to it was a beautiful mahogany dresser topped with photographs in silver frames, porcelain figurines, and a Victrola with a tall stack of 78 rpm records.

"And would you like to practice while you're here?"

Lisa didn't know if this was a trick question, or what kind of answer was expected. She decided to speak from her heart.

"I would very much like to, if you—"

"My son plays the piano," Mrs. Cohen said, interrupting.

Lisa hadn't known there was a son. She didn't have the nerve to ask where he was, fearing he was trapped somewhere by the Nazi nightmare.

"He is in London, in a special school, but he'll be coming here soon," Mrs. Cohen explained in a tone that was devoid of affect. "You may practice for an hour when you come home from work, then you must let the others use the living room for their purposes. If you like, you may play popular songs for us on Sunday."

"Thank you, Ma'am."

"Please close the door as you leave," Mrs. Cohen said, and Lisa let herself out.

Aaron, Gunter, and Gina were waiting for her. "What happened?" Gina asked, dying of curiosity.

Lisa feigned a snobbish look of superiority and held out her hand as though she expected them to kiss it. "I will be performing in the main chamber for an hour daily. You may attend if you wish."

"Ooh!" Gina said in mock fury, and chased her up the stairs.

10

*M*ORNINGS WERE HURRIED. Gina and Lisa developed a routine of holding each other's places in line for the bathroom, then dashing in together to spend as much time as possible in front of the mirror before the other girls banged on the door. Gina showed Lisa how to achieve the fashionable pin curls that would best survive the scarves and hairnets required at the factory.

At breakfast they drank warm tea and milk and gobbled down bread and jam. Lunch items were laid out, and Mrs. Glazer helped them assemble brown bags to take with them: On lucky days, there were cookies or shortbread as a bonus.

Platz & Sons was organized by floor, women's garments on the third, men's on the second, offices on the first.

Lisa was assigned to men's trousers, considered a good place for a beginner. She was surprised by the speed of the work, having been used to her father's meticulous style of double stitching and finished seams. Clearly, the goal at

Platz & Sons was quantity, not quality. Lisa was given the machine next to Mrs. McRae, a quiet woman who patiently explained the intricacies of the job.

Panels of fabric were stacked on her left, and she was to sew them together exactly three-quarters of an inch from the edge. Every panel was exactly the same size and exactly the same color. If she went too slowly, there would be a pileup.

As Mrs. McRae put it: "Mr. Dimble will be here quicker than you can skin a cat, and you'll be in for it."

By the end of a day, Lisa's arms ached and her fingers were sore, but she was grateful that the difficult work demanded her total attention—that way she had no time to worry obsessively about her family or whether a sponsor for Sonia had been found.

Later in the week, Lisa decided to go by Bloomsbury House in the West End. Gina came along to window-shop on Oxford Street; her favorite store was Harvey Nichols, where window after window of elegant mannequins with cigarette holders gazed out arrogantly at passersby.

Lisa loved the hats. "Ooh, that's the one I want," she cooed to Gina, eyeing a soft felt masterpiece with a swooping brim, which projected forward over the mannequin's forehead. A matching-color cord tied in the back. It was the essence of chic. She read aloud from the card at the base: The hat was called "the Margo" and came in "Amethyst, Eau-de-Nil, and Dawn."

"What does that mean?" Lisa asked.

"Purple, green, and tan, silly."

"Why don't they just say that?"

"Because it's fashion. Don't you know anything?" Gina scoffed, happy to enjoy a moment of superiority.

*   *   *

The chaos at Bloomsbury House was still in full swing. More children were arriving on the twice weekly trains— almost ten thousand had come already. Young boys in tweed jackets and ties and girls clutching dolls wandered the hallways. Lisa was again assured that Sonia was on the list, but there was still no word on a sponsor.

Mr. Hardesty's secretary handed her a letter that had just arrived from Vienna—the stamp on the front had a picture of Adolf Hitler. Lisa quickly ripped into the envelope, both to get to the cherished letter within and to destroy the picture of that hateful man.

"Dear Liseleh," she read in her mother's familiar handwriting, "I am afraid I have no good news to report, except that, other than your father's arthritis, we are in good health. Sonia is anxious to join you soon, and it is with difficulty that we have patience to await our turn for the train. Rosie and Leo, too, are trying to come up with plans to join you. I pray they succeed. I hope you are practicing your music. I will send remembrances from home so you do not forget us. Love, Mama."

Tears were running down Lisa's cheeks. Forget them! How could she forget them? They were her very soul.

That night, Lisa sat next to Gunter and Gina at dinner, and they saw how worried and withdrawn she looked.

"Are you all right?" Gunter asked.

"All I can think about is how to help my sister get a sponsor, but I don't know what to do!"

"Where is she?" Gunter asked.

"She's still in Vienna." She hadn't wanted to speak too much about her problems, because she knew that everyone had terrible problems and worries just like hers. "She has a place on the train, but they haven't found a sponsor."

"You should do what Paul did," Gunter said. "Paul! Come here!" he shouted down the table. The blond boy hurried over and squeezed in beside them. "Tell Lisa about your idea." Gunter turned to Lisa and explained, "Paul's brother is still in Munich."

"I went through the phone book for people with my same last name, then rang them up."

"Why?" Lisa asked, not yet understanding.

"I told them I thought they are my relatives! Who knows, maybe they are."

Lisa's eyes lit up. What a good idea! She would try it immediately. After hurrying through dinner, Gunter, Gina, Paul, and Lisa huddled over the heavy phone books of London northwest.

"Mueller," Paul said, paging through the directory. "I looked it up first with the 'e' and then without." He showed Lisa the twenty listings he had underlined. "I called them all. I have two appointments to visit on Saturday."

"But what did you tell them?"

"I said I thought they might be my third cousins!"

"But they're not," Gina said.

"Of course not, but I get to see them, and maybe they'll like me."

Lisa quickly turned to the Js, Jura. Dragging her finger down the page, she found a Juracek, and then several Justices—there were no Juras in this part of London.

Aaron came in the room, leaned over the phone directory with them, and listened for a moment. "Try Y instead of J. People change the spelling sometimes."

She turned quickly to the last page; there was nothing between Young and Yusef.

"Maybe we could counterfeit an affidavit," Aaron offered.

"How would you know how to do that?" Gina asked suspiciously.

"There are ways," he answered with a look that allowed no further questions.

The talk of counterfeiting reminded Lisa of Michael, the boy she had befriended on the train, who spoke so much of Sherlock Holmes. She remembered the two huge fur coats that surrounded him at the train station and figured his sponsors were rich—what was his name? Her mind was a blank. Then suddenly she saw the image of poor cousin Sid on the platform and her face brightened.

"Wait! My father's cousin! Danziger! We could look for the cousin's name!"

There were plenty of Danzigers in the phone book, especially in the predominantly Jewish neighborhood nearby, Golders Green.

"I'll help," Aaron offered gallantly.

"So will I," said Gina.

"Me too," Gunter chimed in.

"We'll each call four of these numbers tomorrow," Gina offered.

"And on Saturday Gunter will go with Paul, in case he needs help, all right?"

Lisa wrote down the phone numbers and handed them out. She decided that she would visit the four closest Danzigers in person, since she didn't trust her English to the telephone.

"I love being part of a team!" Lisa said, overcome with excitement.

"We'll call ourselves the Committee for the Resolution of All Ills," Aaron pronounced.

Aaron put his hand in the middle of the table, and Gina, Paul, Gunter, and Lisa put their hands on the top.

"We're the committee, right?"

"The committee we are!"

Lisa received permission from Mrs. Cohen to switch her practicing to the hour after dinner, so she could spend time after work canvassing the neighborhoods. She loved having a plan, and memorized a little speech for herself, resolving to leave no stone unturned—she'd get Sonia out no matter what.

Knocking on doors proved more tiring than she had anticipated. None of the Danzigers said yes. The petite, determined figure in her neat pleated skirt walked up and down the streets of Golders Green, knocking on every door she could, but the answer was always the same: "We wish we could help, but . . ." These doors had been knocked on many times before, she realized; there had been many refugees before her.

It wasn't just that families didn't want to take an extra child, it was that the children of London themselves were being organized to evacuate. Houses were being boarded up and toddlers were being shipped to the country.

Sometimes, as Lisa made the clanking noise to unlatch a gate, she could see a person in the upper story lift a curtain and peer out. The shade would then be drawn, the bell not answered. They knew in advance what the pretty young girl would ask them and couldn't bear to say no again.

The newsboys called out the evening's headlines, which always included the words *Hitler* or *Poland*. Sandbags were piling up in front of store windows; there was a sense of urgency in the air.

Lisa had begged the people at work, but they were all as poor as she was. She knocked on shops near the factory, and never thought of giving up; she just resolved to approach things more systematically. She would find every Danziger in London if that was what it took.

When her stomach told her it was dinnertime, she would find the nearest underground station and make her way back to Willesden Green station. At the fish and chips shop, she picked up her pace so as not to be tempted to spend any of the few shillings she had saved.

After dinner Lisa would go to the piano, happy to lose herself in music. The late summer evenings were long and warm, and the large bay windows were left open onto the front lawn. Neighbors and passersby enjoyed a concert of classical culture from old world Vienna.

Before the evening was over, the five friends, Paul, Gunter, Aaron, Lisa, and Gina, would have a "committee meeting." Paul reported that he had secured a sponsor for his little brother, but that so far there were no seats available on the Berlin Kindertransport—too many families were fighting for a chance to save their children.

Lisa had the opposite problem—a space on the train and still no sponsor.

At the end of yet another unproductive afternoon, Lisa walked up Riffel Road with her head bowed, on her way back to the hostel. A voice stopped her.

"Young lady, come here a moment. Please."

It was the strange neighbor lady in black, leaning on a large wooden-handled rake. With her long dress and high-button shoes, she looked like the witch in Grimms' fairy tales.

"I have too many cucumbers and tomatoes this week, would thee take them to Mrs. Cohen for me on your way?"

"Of course," Lisa said politely, surprised at the strange English.

"I'll get thee a bag. Please start under there," she said, pointing to a dark green plant. Lisa hesitantly lifted the large leaves and was surprised to find half a dozen cucumbers waiting. She snapped them off and piled them on the lawn next to a neat stack of already picked tomatoes.

The woman still hadn't come back. Lisa waited. Overcome by temptation, she reached for a juicy tomato, and bit in. The woman came out the door just as the warm juice exploded over Lisa's chin and blouse.

"My, my! Look at thee!"

It was just an overripe tomato, but after a day of frustration and exhaustion, and doors shut in her face, Lisa couldn't control herself and burst into tears.

"It's nothing to worry about, I'll get thee a towel."

When the woman returned, Lisa was still crying. She was ashamed of her tears in front of this stranger, but no matter how hard she tried, she couldn't stop sobbing.

"You poor dear. Things must be so difficult . . . difficult for all of thee," the lady said kindly, making Lisa cry even harder.

The woman handed her a plain handkerchief, and Lisa gradually calmed herself.

"Tell me, what's the matter, dear?" the lady asked with concern.

Lisa didn't say anything right away, afraid she would start to cry again, but finally she found a voice. "My sister is still in Vienna. Please, please, do you know anyone that could help us be a sponsor?"

* * *

The woman's name was Mrs. Canfield. She wasn't the scary or strange specter Lisa had thought, but a Quaker, a member of the Religious Society of Friends. She listened carefully to Lisa's painful pleading, then promised to do all she could. She explained a bit of Quaker philosophy to Lisa, who was in no shape to understand it.

Accepting the handkerchief she was offered as a gift, Lisa backed out the door, carrying the vegetables up the street with a glimmer of hope in her heart.

Two days later, Mr. Hardesty called to leave word that a Quaker family in the north of England had agreed to sponsor Sonia and that expedited calls were being made to the Jewish Refugee Agency in Vienna. Sonia would be on the train within the week, and Lisa was delirious with joy.

The next day was Friday, September 1, 1939, and Lisa came home early for Shabbat. After the lighting of the candles, Mrs. Glazer read aloud from the air raid precautions pamphlet that had been delivered to the hostel that afternoon. The total blackout of London had been ordered. In anticipation of the bombing, bolts of black cloth were to be made into curtains and hung in the windows so no light would shine through. Gas masks previously stored in the basement were to be placed at the head of each person's bed.

When the sun set that evening, no streetlights came on. Everyone gathered around the radio, which Mrs. Cohen had switched on in spite of the fact that it was the Sabbath. The sad, hushed children listened as the BBC reported that one million Nazi soldiers had marched across the border from Germany to Poland in the last twenty-four hours, with lightning speed, headed for Warsaw. A new word was added to the vocabulary—blitzkrieg.

Lisa went to sleep overwrought with worry, lying awake

to the sounds of several children crying in the bedrooms down the hall. She thought of only one thing: Would Sonia make it?

The busy preparations continued the next morning. Lisa was hemming the curtains in the living room as Edith and Gina answered the doorbell. They greeted three of the nuns from the convent next door, who brought boxes filled with tins of food.

"We're cleaning out the larder. We've been ordered to evacuate," one of them explained.

"Thank you very much, sisters," Mrs. Cohen said, coming up behind the girls.

"We would prefer to stay, but I'm afraid the bishop doesn't see it our way. We'd like to offer you the use of our basement, if you'd like. The air raid warden says it's the best basement on the block for a bomb shelter. Oh, and if anyone could find it in his heart to water the hyacinths for us, Sister Agnes would be most grateful."

Mrs. Cohen thanked the sisters profusely, while Lisa helped carry the tins of sardines and meats to Mrs. Glazer, who read the labels, checking for nonkosher ingredients.

When she came back to the foyer, the nuns were leaving. One turned back and addressed Lisa. "We'd like to thank you for the beautiful music, we'll miss it."

"Thank you," Lisa said, blushing.

"Miss Jura, will you come with me to my room?" Mrs. Cohen said, closing the door.

As she entered, Lisa noticed that the figurines and framed photographs were neatly wrapped and packed in boxes for protection from the possibility of bombing.

"I understand your sister is to arrive today," she said, shutting the door to the inner sanctum.

"Yes, ma'am."

"Mr. Hardesty called me to discuss where to send you. I understand that Mrs. Canfield has friends who will take Sonia, but that it might be difficult for them to take you as well."

In the frantic emotions of the past few days, Lisa hadn't even thought about her own future. Things had happened too fast to allow herself the luxury of plans and expectations. She'd almost forgotten that her stay at Willesden Lane was to be temporary.

Mrs. Cohen continued: "I told him that we would be willing to keep you here, even though we'll only be allowed thirty ration books and you would be our thirty-second person. We'd be willing to tighten our belts a little bit, if you'd like to stay."

Lisa bowed her head in gratitude and to hide the tears that were being shed all too often. She nodded yes. "Thank you very much," she whispered.

"That's settled, then. Please close the door behind you."

Lisa went to the door, but Mrs. Cohen called her back. "Wait a moment," she said, opening the doors of the mahogany dresser and lifting out a stack of sheet music. "Would you like to borrow this?"

Lisa's eyes widened at the sight. It was Chopin and Schubert and Tchaikovsky! A name was penciled neatly on the top of each book: "Hans Cohen."

"Thank you so much, ma'am," she cried.

Sonia was due to arrive on the 3:22 train at the Liverpool station that afternoon.

The train station was a madhouse. As fate would have it, the children of London were being evacuated that very weekend, and long lines of English toddlers were being organized by their parents and volunteers. They had tiny packs strapped to their backs and white paper identification tags fastened with strong twine through buttonholes.

A sign outside the station read: "Southern Railways Special Announcement: Sept 1,2,3 the following steam trains are required for the evacuation of children and will not be available for ordinary passengers: 9:30 A.M., 11:30 A.M., etc. all weekend long."

Lisa located the volunteers from the Bloomsbury House, and they helped her to find Mr. and Mrs. Bates from Norwich, who also spoke with the odd-sounding thees and thous. They offered reassuring words about their farm and about their daughter, who was also Sonia's age, and together they went to look for the special train coming in on track sixteen.

The waiting was an agony for Lisa, but finally the children began to emerge from the Kindertransport. The boys were dressed as Lisa remembered, in their finest wool suits and tiny ties; the girls in woolen dresses. In comparison with the lines of bright-eyed English children she'd seen outside (who had been promised a vacation in the countryside), these girls and boys looked exhausted and terrified.

Sonia was wearing her heavy maroon coat, even though the weather was warm. When Lisa saw the frail and serious thirteen-year-old come down the steep steps, she thought she would crumple on the spot from the rush of emotion and relief. Breaking away from the couple, she ran to meet Sonia, grabbing her tightly in her arms, calling her name over and over. "Sonia, Sonia, you've come, Sonia." Again she was sobbing and couldn't make her voice utter any of the words she had been preparing.

For a long moment they held each other, and it almost seemed she was home in Vienna again.

Lisa had told herself to be strong and positive to show her sister that everything would be all right, so she forced herself to stop crying. Mr. and Mrs. Bates had tickets on the train back to the north of England, which would leave from Paddington station in two hours, and they'd been lucky to get any seats at all. Lisa was desperate to make good use of every second of the thirty minutes they had been given for their reunion. The two sisters embraced all the way to the first-class café on the second floor of the station, where they were left alone for a private reunion. Grasping her pale sister's hand on top of the white tablecloth, Lisa called the waiter, proudly showing off her English by ordering tea and sandwiches. Sonia politely nibbled at the unfamiliar food, while Lisa opened the package that her sister had brought her from Vienna. Her heart leapt to her throat. Inside was a silver lamé evening purse that had belonged to Malka's grandmother and a book of preludes by Chopin—the one her mother had helped her learn. It seemed like yesterday. She was overwhelmed by emotion.

Opening the letter from her mother, she read: "Your father and I are so comforted to know that you and Sonia are both at last safe in England away from the dreadful place that our home has become. We are putting every effort now to find a way to get Rosie out. Take good care of our littlest treasure, Lisa, and know that all our prayers are for the day when we will be reunited."

Attached to the letter was a photograph of Abraham. She was so grateful to have his picture—for try as she might, it was harder and harder to remember all the details of his beloved face. She stared at the photograph and was shocked to see that his hair was now totally white.

The thirty minutes passed in a heartbeat, and Mr. and

Mrs. Bates returned. Standing up regretfully, Lisa embraced her sister, trying to reassure the trembling child.

"The minute the bombing is over, you'll come to London with me, I promise."

Sonia was too frightened and emotional to respond in words. She clung to her older sister's hand while Lisa helped with the difficult separation, taking Sonia's suitcase and handing it to Mr. Bates.

"I'm so sorry, but we mustn't be late for the train," Mrs. Bates said, taking Sonia's hand.

"I promise! Sonia," Lisa cried reassuringly as the three of them walked away. She watched them disappear, then broke down, tired of being brave beyond her years.

The next morning, at eleven-fifteen, the residents of 243 Willesden Lane put aside their chores and huddled again around the wireless to hear Prime Minister Chamberlain announce formally what everyone had long suspected—that Britain was declaring war on Germany. "It is evil things that we shall be fighting against—brute force, bad faith, injustice, suppression, and persecution, and against them I am certain that the right will prevail."

Lisa sat on the couch next to Johnny, reassured by the weight of his large, strong presence but wishing she were as certain as the voice on the radio that "right would prevail." She had mixed feelings about the coming of war— hopefully it would mean an end to the Nazis and would mean that she could return home. But when would that be, what would happen to her family in the meantime? Looking around the room at the worried faces, she knew that everyone shared her feelings—and that in their hearts they feared things would get worse before they got better.

* * *

The rest of the day was spent preparing a bomb shelter in the basement of the convent next door. Everyone pitched in, carrying sandbags and buckets of earth to use in case of fire and stocking the cellar with first aid supplies—the packages of antiburn cream, plasters, and bandages. Finally they dragged down their mattresses and linens and set up cozy corners to sleep in.

So they could have a second entrance to the convent, the boys made an opening in the fence, careful not to trample the hyacinths that Sister Agnes so loved.

At six o'clock they were called again around the radio. This time it was King George who spoke: "It is unthinkable that we should refuse to meet this challenge . . . to this high purpose I now call my people at home and my peoples across the seas. I ask them to stand firm and united in this time of trial." His voice was more soothing than Chamberlain's, and Lisa wondered secretly where the princess was and what she was doing.

Mrs. Cohen rarely spoke after the broadcasts, but tonight she switched off the wireless and stood up awkwardly. "Please, listen for a moment, children. I know you might be frightened, but it is now more important than ever for you to be courageous. You must try your best to be examples for the others around you here in Britain. Let us say a prayer of gratitude to the good people who have taken us into their country and help them in any way we can—especially by being extra obedient and courteous. We will go about our daily activities—you will go to your jobs as before, and we will put our trust in God."

Lisa looked over at Paul, whose face was drawn and lifeless. He'd been given the news that afternoon that no more transports would be allowed to leave "greater Germany." No more sisters and brothers would be coming until the end of the war.

Lisa had been the lucky one—Sonia had arrived on the very last train.

11

BRITAIN READIED itself for the German attack. Posters were slapped on subway walls, some showing dashing air force pilots in leather jackets, others showing German soldiers parachuting from the sky—"How to Recognize the Enemy," they said, and described the German eagle-wing insignias to watch out for. Londoners walked around looking up, convinced the Nazis would be arriving at any moment.

The London Zoo brought its animals inside, stuffing boa constrictors and cheetahs into sturdy crates. Antiaircraft guns were set up in Hyde Park, and in a confusing attempt to throw the enemy off guard, road signs were uprooted throughout the city. Lisa was grateful she already knew her way around.

The assembly line at Platz & Sons was immediately switched over to the full-time production of uniforms, and Lisa's floor now cut and stitched trousers for the Royal Navy. Flared bell-bottoms flew out of her machine, and she let her mind wander to the brave midshipmen who would soon be wearing them. Perhaps even Monty would get a pair.

One day, Mrs. McRae, the line manager, seemed less chatty than usual, and at lunch, Lisa overheard the other girls talking about the news.

"Mr. McRae has been shipped to France already! Did you hear? Last night, real sudden-like, with no warning at all. For God's sake, don't they have any concern for the missuses?"

"Now, how are they going to keep a secret if we know about it? U-boats'd get 'em 'fore you count to ten."

"Guess you're right. But they're going to smash them stinkin' Jerries, aren't they. It'll be over before Easter."

Lisa listened to their conversation but didn't feel enough at ease to join in. They talked so fast with their Cockney accents, it was all she could do to catch half of what they said. She imagined the dark expanse of the English Channel, the gray sky she had seen almost a year ago now, and pictured the men setting out to sea.

She was so grateful they were going; she'd sew a million uniforms for them if that's what was needed!

Now that she'd become a permanent member of the hostel, Lisa was given her own drawer in the bureau which she filled with her music, the hairnets she needed for the factory, and several new scarves that she had sewn for herself during lunch break. The scarves were just pieces of cloth she had rescued from the boxes of donated clothes, but they gave her a fashionable flair, and made her think of her older sister, Rosie. Rosie! Where was her beautiful older sister now? Was she safe?

The hour from six to seven was a favorite time for

everyone to gather in the living room and listen to Lisa practice. Since the gift of Mrs. Cohen's sheet music, she no longer had to play only the pieces she knew by heart. Part of every session was an adventurous struggle through difficult new pieces, and she longed for her mother's guidance. When the effort to learn something new was too tiring for her already exhausted fingers, she would lapse into her favorite, the Grieg piano concerto. She played the unforgettable first bars, Dum dum, da dum dum, and invariably, someone from the "committee" would hum the musical response: Dum dum dum da dum. The heroic and tender passages of the Grieg piano concerto had worked their way inside everyone's heads, and the musical response to the opening bars had become the call to arms for a committee meeting. Aaron had been the first to do it, and the habit had stuck.

Sometimes, Gunter would sit on the piano bench to be closer to the beautiful music. His round, horn-rimmed glasses made him look a bit like a junior version of Professor Isseles. As Lisa had gotten to know Gunter, she had come to love his sweet and gentle manner. He had grown up in Cologne, where his father had owned a hardware shop, and he loved to play chess. Lisa liked his company on the bench and sometimes shared the images of the music that her mother had instilled in her.

"Hear that? That's the sound of the deep blue of the fjords."

Gunter smiled.

"Grieg was from Norway, so I picture this as a summer's night when the sun never sets. Can you see it? Low in the sky." She played the end of the elegant slow movement, then exhaled quickly and launched into a staccato dance.

"Ta ta ti da, ta ta ti da," she hummed along. "Those are the peasants dancing."

"Must be exhausting," Gunter said, making her laugh.

Promptly at seven Mrs. Glazer announced dinner, and the children rushed to the dining room. As Lisa tidied up her music, she noticed that Johnny "King Kong" still sat in the corner. She looked over at him, and he put his note-book down and clapped. She smiled back and hurried to join the others.

Gina's and Lisa's beds were next to each other, and the two girls whispered confidences after lights out. One night Gina suddenly asked, "Have you ever had a boyfriend?"

"Of course not!" Lisa blurted out honestly.

"I did," Gina said in a conspiratorial voice.

"In Vienna?"

"Uh huh."

"What was his name?" Lisa asked, riveted.

"Walter."

"Did he get out, too?"

"He didn't have to. He wasn't Jewish."

"You had a gentile boyfriend?" Lisa asked, scandalized.

"Why shouldn't I?"

Lisa didn't say anything. Sometimes Gina was too con-fusing to her.

Gina continued her story. "He came to the train to say good-bye and brought me a flower."

Suddenly Gina bounded out of bed and fumbled through a drawer in the dark, coming up with a sweet-smelling box. Lisa peered at it through the almost total darkness but made out the form of a dried flower.

"I can still see him standing there when I left. His pants

were really wide and they were flapping in the wind—they made so much noise."

"Do you miss him?" Lisa asked.

"Not really. I don't really remember what he looks like anymore," came the matter-of-fact answer. Gone was the scattered gossipy air about Gina that had bothered Lisa in the beginning. Now they were closer than ever—she had found "a best friend," someone to help fill the hole of not having her sisters near her.

"Do you like Gunter?" Lisa ventured.

"I don't know. He seems kind of soft."

"Maybe that's a good thing. I bet you he'll make a lot of money when he gets older."

"You think so?"

As the girls whispered, they heard humming coming from outside the door and down the stairs—it was unmistakable.

"Dum, dum, da dum, dum." The opening bars of the Grieg!

Shivering in delight, they scuttled out of bed, trying not to wake Edith as they slipped their coats over their nightgowns and jammed their bare feet into their shoes.

The humming came again, followed by a quick whistle. Tiptoeing down the stairs into the dark foyer, they saw the front door was open. Gunter and Aaron were standing on the porch, peering at the sky through binoculars.

"What are you doing?" Gina asked excitedly.

"We're spotting German planes," Gunter said with importance.

"Follow us! Quick!" Aaron said, sticking a matchbook in the door as it closed so it wouldn't lock them out.

"It's after curfew," Lisa whispered.

"We're official plane spotters, come on, hurry up."

"Where did you get the binoculars?" Lisa asked, not convinced.

"I can't tell you."

"Ooh, don't say that, it makes me nervous!"

"We got them from the air raid warden. We've been asking every night, and finally he let us be spotters," said Gunter.

The girls were led to the unlocked front door of the convent next door and up two flights of stairs. A ladder lay waiting under an open hatch, and they clambered through it onto a large flat portion of the slate roof.

"*Mein Gott im Himmel!*" Lisa exclaimed, looking up at the extraordinary sight. The blackout of London had produced a wondrous celestial show rivaling the greatest planetarium. The moon had not yet risen, and the white band of the Milky Way seemed close enough to touch; the brightest stars twinkled like fairy dust.

Aaron got proudly to work. There were several blankets on the roof already, and he stretched one out and lay down, putting the field glasses to his eyes.

"We're looking for two kinds of bombers, the Dornier Do 17 and the Heinkel He 111," he said, scouring the heavens.

"Well, aren't you Mr. Know-it-all?" said Gina.

"The Dornier looks like a pencil, the Heinkel is rounder."

Gunter spread out another blanket and all four of them lay side by side, looking straight up into the sky.

Nothing moved. They looked and looked.

"What happens if you see something?" Gina asked.

"You blow this whistle and the block air raid warden will hear you."

Gina and Lisa shared an impressed look.

"Let me try," Lisa said.

Aaron handed her the binoculars and showed her how to focus. She put them to her eyes and waved them around unprofessionally.

"You look like you're chasing mosquitoes."

Lisa slowed her motion and her vision came to rest on a close-up of a human face. She screamed, dropping the glasses. Everyone stared in the direction of her gaze. A neighbor, perched on the roof three houses over, waved at them. All of London was pitching in.

From then on, the "committee" met on the roof every Tuesday and Thursday. Sometimes Paul joined them, but often not; he had become more withdrawn since the failure to get his brother out of Germany. Lisa worried about him.

"Go back and get Paul," she pressed Aaron as they trekked across the lawn.

"Oh, let him sleep," Aaron said.

"No! I want you to get him."

"I'll go," offered Gunter, ever the gentleman.

One night it was colder than usual, and all five huddled close under blankets.

The evening's chatter was usually organized by Gina, who either told gossip from the factory, made observations about the royal family, or introduced a challenge, as she did tonight.

"Let's each tell something embarrassing."

Gunter groaned. "You go first."

"All right, I will." Gina launched into a rambling account of the time when she'd been a servant and had made some arcane faux pas that the others didn't understand. Her stories always ended by making the point that her family was very wealthy and she knew more about silver service in particular or culture in general than the English upper class.

"That's not embarrassing," complained Lisa.

"Then you tell us something," Gina countered.

"Remember I told you about the castle? I was caught once throwing out the nappies, because they were so disgusting I was going to vomit."

"You already told me about that, it doesn't count!" Gina said.

"I'll tell you something," Aaron said, his voice taking on a seriousness it usually didn't have. "I'll tell you something, if you want."

"Of course we do," said Gina.

Aaron rolled onto his back, staring into the sky.

"When I first came to England, I was sent to a little town near the Scottish border—to work in the stables. It turned out the lady who sponsored me had a little dairy farm. It was freezing all the time. I had to sleep in the barn on a cot, but I piled straw all around it, so I guess it wasn't so bad. When everyone was called up, her husband joined the army—the day after he left she had me move inside."

Aaron paused, as if he wondered whether to continue.

"And?" asked Paul.

"She didn't want me to move the cot inside though, she wanted me to sleep in her bed."

The words fell heavily on Lisa; she didn't know why but she didn't want to hear what came next. Aaron sensed the mood of the group and went silent.

"Did you sleep with her?" Paul insisted.

Aaron didn't answer for a long time, as if he wished he could take it all back. "What do you think?" he tried to say ambiguously, but the friends looked at this handsome, arrogant boy and knew the answer.

Lisa didn't know whether she liked this Aaron anymore. Why had he shared this? It made her uneasy.

Gunter had been listening quietly; there were tears in his eyes.

"Gunter! What's the matter?" Gina asked gently.

"I was thinking about the birds and bees—when my father tried to tell me about the facts of life," he answered, his voice trailing off.

"And?" Gina asked.

Gunter was silent.

"Oh, please tell us," she coaxed.

"It was the day I was to leave Cologne. The transport left at midnight, so there was a lot of time after dinner, and my mother asked him, just like that. She said, "Take your son and tell him what fathers tell sons.' So we left the house and started walking around the block. My father hadn't spoken much since we'd decided about the Kindertransport . . . he had been awarded the Iron Cross in the Great War, fighting for Germany, and now they'd smashed his shop and were sending me away."

Gunter started to cry.

"What did he say?" Gina asked.

"He never said anything because he couldn't stop crying."

Gina took his hand and squeezed it tight.

As weeks passed and there was no sign of Germans, the chill of winter made the rooftop adventure less attractive, so the Willesden boys gave the binoculars back to the warden. Months went by without the sighting of a single German bomber, and many Britons became convinced it had all been a false alarm. Half of the 800,000 parents with young children who had left for the countryside returned home and England played a waiting game. Even the 150,000 soldiers of the British Expeditionary Force, who had been sent across the Channel, were waiting, hunkered down in muddy barns in Belgium and France.

One day, Mrs. Cohen asked the *Kinder* to move their bedding back to the hostel from the convent bomb shelter, and the normal life of the hostel resumed—if anyone dared call it that.

Lisa's waiting also continued. When Hanukkah came, a promised visit from Sonia was postponed. In spite of the lull, people said London was still too dangerous.

12

$\mathcal{R}$ATIONING WAS announced New Year's Day. It was 1940. Mrs. Cohen sorted through the coupons on the kitchen counter and muttered to Mrs. Glazer, "Four ounces of meat per week per person? Good grief, these are growing boys and girls."

She took the coupons to the shops on Walm Lane twice a week to pick up the meager supplies. Luckily, the kosher butcher kept a jar on the counter with a hand-lettered sign—"For Our Needy Refugees"—and used the coins to help the hostel buy additional provisions; occasionally, the greengrocer slipped in something extra. All in all, they got by.

The bulk of the items were parsnips, potatoes, and flour. The children were assigned turns lugging the heavy bags back home, moaning about the disappearance of candy and chocolate from their lives. The rations were mere subsistence; Lisa often felt hunger gnawing at her stomach.

One Saturday, when it was Lisa's and Gina's turn, a

freak snowstorm transformed the neighborhood from its customary gray to a brilliant white. After synagogue, the two girls broke off from the rest of the group and went to collect the groceries, fastening the bags onto rickety-wheeled trolleys. The sun was shining for a change, and Lisa saw things in the neighborhood she had never noticed before.

There were colorful, reflective strips in the shape of wrenches and hammers pasted on the blackout curtains of the hardware store, and the bric-a-brac shop had a hand-painted mural of a room of antiques. The light stanchions had newly painted zebra stripes to ward off the rash of car accidents that had begun the night the streetlights were turned off. It all put her into a merry mood, and the two girls skidded home on the icy sidewalks, laughing their way down Willesden Lane into the gigantic crossfire of a serious snowball fight.

The hostel had divided up into teams by rooms, and the boys and girls were pelting each other mercilessly. Lisa and Gina became instant fodder for the cannonballs of snow, so they were forced to fight back with everything they had—turnips and potatoes (the vegetables flew better and took less time to produce than snowballs)—and soon several of the little boys were sobbing from direct hits.

"I'm sorry, Leo! I didn't mean it," Lisa said with contrition, but ten-year-old Leo responded by stuffing a huge wad of snow down her back.

"Truce!" someone yelled, and Johnny came forward and comforted the crying children by rolling an enormous snowball and beginning a snowman. Everyone pitched in and the snowball became life-size. Gina hit upon the idea of decorating the face with a green turnip top. She stuck it on to make a mustache, and everybody gasped.

"*Der Führer* has arrived," she said in an eerie voice.

"Let's kill him!" someone shouted.

The younger boys leapt on the snowman, and in seconds the effigy was pummeled into slush.

The front door opened and Mrs. Cohen came out on the porch and surveyed the soggy groceries with displeasure. Turnips and potatoes littered the front yard, and her expression alone was enough to send everyone scurrying to pick them up.

"Aaron, Paul? Please come here for a moment."

Mrs. Cohen was carrying a bucket of black tar and handed it to them. "Mrs. Knight at 156 would like our help, her roof is leaking. I want you two boys to find a brush and help her."

Paul took the pail from her, but Aaron hung back, saying to no one in particular, "Isn't it convenient to have all these refugees to work all the time."

Mrs. Cohen overheard and turned to him. "Aaron, I'm tired of your thinking that you are somehow above these things. And I'm also tired of your thinking you don't have to obey the same rules as everyone else. If you are late for a meal one more time without a good excuse, we will not serve you, understood?"

Aaron pretended he wasn't affected by her words and turned and left with Paul. Lisa watched him and worried. What worried her most was that she liked him too much. He was trouble; and she knew she should stay away.

Lisa and Gina hurried to finish kitchen duty, carrying the soggy bags of produce to Mrs. Glazer in the kitchen.

"Downstairs, please, but leave some potatoes here," the cook said to Gina, directing her to the tiny cellar below.

"Here, Lisa," she said, handing her a large knife. "Peel me fifteen potatoes, would you, please?"

Lisa was beginning her task as Mrs. Cohen came into the kitchen. She stared at Lisa's snow-reddened hands holding the poised knife.

"She is not to use knives, Mrs. Glazer," the matron said matter-of-factly, handing the sharp utensil back to the cook. "Please come here, Lisa, I want to introduce you to someone."

Mrs. Cohen escorted Lisa to the living room, past several girls who were vacuuming and dusting, over to a boy in his early teens who sat calmly on the couch. He had neatly combed hair and was wearing dark glasses.

"This is my son, Hans. He was hoping you could play something for him."

"Hello," Lisa said shyly.

"He will be staying at the hostel with us," Mrs. Cohen added with her usual formality, then turned and left them alone.

"Thank you for the use of your music; I hope you didn't mind," Lisa said.

"Not a problem. I won't be needing it," he said with an odd sarcasm. "Would you play something by Debussy?"

"'Clair de Lune'?" she offered.

"How about 'The Girl with the Flaxen Hair'?" he replied.

"I don't know it."

"There is a copy of the music there."

"I'm terrible at sight-reading."

"Please?" he asked.

Trapped, Lisa leafed through the stack of music and found the piece. She hated to sight-read because she was so bad at it, but fortunately the piece was simple, and she muddled through the first page. When she saw the complicated second page she stopped, too much of a perfectionist to allow herself any more mistakes. "I'll play you the 'Clair de Lune.'" Without waiting for a response, she launched into her favorite piece.

"Mother was right, you play beautifully—it almost makes me feel there might be something nice left in the world," Hans said when it was over. He had a sad, resigned air about him.

"Won't you play me something now?" she asked.

There was a long silence before he spoke. "Yes, I will, if you'll help me to the piano."

It was only then that she realized Hans was blind. She got up, took him by the arm, and led him to the piano.

"Please show me middle C."

She put his thumb on the proper key, then hesitantly, he began "The Girl with the Flaxen Hair," playing with warmth and determination. "I'm sorry, but it's the only piece I remember by heart."

Listening to him play, a profound feeling overtook her. How lucky I am, she thought. She had spent so much time thinking about how terrible things were and how worried she felt about her parents and Rosie that she hadn't had time to be grateful—grateful for Sonia's escape, grateful for her own freedom. She knew God had given her a gift, and she vowed to use this gift to its fullest. She would practice and practice; she would fulfill the promise she had made to her mother.

13

ANS SPENT his days in the living room, reading books in braille and listening to the wireless, memorizing the voices of every reporter and politician on the BBC. His only respite was Lisa's practice session. Each evening when she returned from work, he happily joined her at the piano bench, tapping his cane to the rhythm of her Czerny exercises and offering praise and suggestions with each new piece she'd tackle.

After each session he returned again to the radio. The recent news had been grim. The arrival of spring had brought an end to the waiting—in quick succession the Nazis had landed in Norway, invaded the Netherlands, and entered Belgium, Luxembourg, and the north of France. The new vocabulary word was *Sichelschnitt*, the cut of the sickle; Hitler's panzer divisions were slicing through Europe.

The third Sunday in May, Hans spread the word that there would be an important broadcast that evening, the first speech by the new prime minister. Almost all of the thirty residents crowded into the living room, spilling over the sofas and onto the floor, as Hans turned up the volume.

Winston Churchill's voice was powerful and magnetic, and they leaned forward to hear every word. "I speak to you for the first time as Prime Minister in a solemn hour for the life of our country. . . . A tremendous battle is raging in France and Flanders. The Germans, by a remarkable combination of air bombing and heavily armored tanks, have broken though the French defenses north of the Maginot Line, and strong columns of their armored vehicles are ravaging the open country. . . . They have penetrated deeply and spread alarm and confusion in their tracks. . . . It would be foolish to disguise the gravity of the hour. It would be still more foolish to lose heart and courage . . . for myself I have invincible confidence in the French army and its leaders. . . ."

When Lisa went to bed that night she was trembling with fear. She pulled out the pictures of her mother and her father and held them close to her as she fell asleep.

Two weeks later Lisa received two letters. One was from Sonia in Norwich and included a small black-and-white photo of her young sister in a flared wool coat, standing in a garden with her new family and the family dog. "I have enough to eat and am learning to speak English, but I miss you very much and . . ."

The second letter was very disturbing. It was her own letter to her parents in Vienna, addressed to 13 Franzenbrükestrasse, which had been sent back stamped "Undeliverable." Lisa called a "committee" meeting, in despair. Gunter, Gina, Paul, Aaron, and Lisa gathered around the dining table and shared their worries—none of them had received any recent news of their parents. They agreed to meet at the Bloomsbury House the next day after work.

Gina and Lisa met the boys outside the Tottenham Court tube station, and together they walked east to Bloomsbury Street. The beleaguered old building was familiar by now. The Jewish Refugee Agency offices inside were still overcrowded, no longer with lost children, but with desperate relatives searching for news.

The five teenagers convinced the volunteer secretary that they had to see Mr. Hardesty himself, but when they were ushered into his office, they were somewhat tonguetied.

"And how is Willesden Lane?" he asked, recognizing them.

"Mr. Hardesty, we do not have one word from our parents," Lisa said, speaking for the group. "No one is giving us any information."

"The government must know what is happening," said Aaron. "Someone must know."

Mr. Hardesty looked at the visibly shaken teenagers, running his fingers through his thinning white hair. "I don't know what to tell you. Believe me, we know very little. The Red Cross is trying to find out all they can."

Lisa handed Mr. Hardesty a handwritten list of the names of all their parents. "Please, can you find out where they are?"

He took the list of names and read it, then leaned back in his chair and shut his eyes, searching for the right words. "All we know is that many Jews are being sent to relocation camps, and that is why you are not receiving letters."

"Camps?" Gina asked forlornly.

"Relocation camps, we know very little about them. The Red Cross will try to help, but personally I know nothing . . . I'm sorry. Now if there are questions about England I can answer, I'd be—"

Aaron stood up rudely and headed for the door. The rest followed, but Lisa stayed for a second. "Thank you, Mr. Hardesty," she said.

Aaron walked angrily down the hall. "Why would he care, anyway? He's not Jewish!"

Lisa looked in Aaron's eyes and saw how frightened he was. "Let's go for a walk in the park," she offered, trying to comfort him. She had always assumed that nothing bothered him; now she wasn't so sure.

They walked back to the crowded sidewalks of Tottenham Court Road. Aaron pulled a coin from his pocket and led the way to a fish and chips stall, where they were handed steaming hunks of cod in wartime wrapping—recycled newspapers. When they pulled the paper off the fish, the black ink of the headline stained the flesh. Aaron read (backward): "Miracle at Dunkirk."

"Some miracle all right," he mocked. "I don't see why the English are so happy about the miraculous evacuation of hundreds of thousands of soldiers from the beaches of France. It looks like a massive retreat to me."

"Aaron, it is a miracle," Gunter protested. "The Nazis had us surrounded; without the boatlift, they would have captured half the British army!"

Lisa agreed, and so did most of England; Britain was overtaken by a wave of superpatriotism, Union Jacks flew from every door. It made her proud; she only wished she could share the sight with her family to give them hope.

Eager to change the mood of the group, Lisa insisted on going to Hyde Park to see the swans. The ponds were flanked by antiaircraft guns pointed expectantly at the sky.

Gina looked terrible, and her stride had slowed to a morose shuffle. She sat on the park bench and put her head in her hands.

"I know this sounds really selfish, but I can't imagine my mother in a camp. How can she go to a camp? What do they mean, is it like Dovercourt? With tents? She's never even cooked for herself! She doesn't know how to do anything! Maybe they won't take rich people like her. . . . maybe they'll let her bring the maid."

As soon as she said the silly words, she cried again, this time about how stupid she sounded. "I know it sounds stupid, I can't help it," she said.

"No, it doesn't," Gunter said, taking her hand. "Come, let's go feed the swans; it's better not to think about it."

Paul, Lisa, and Aaron wandered around the park.

"Will we always be at war?" Lisa wondered aloud.

"Guess it depends on whether the Yanks get into it, doesn't it?" answered Paul.

"They won't," Aaron said.

"What do you boys want to be when it's over?"

Aaron looked at Lisa strangely. "Who cares? There's a war going on."

"I'm going to join the air force," Paul said, proud to have a better answer than Aaron's.

"No, I mean, what do you want to be after the war . . . what do you want to do with your life?" Lisa insisted.

"I don't know. My father was a shoe salesman," Paul said, somewhat lost.

"Why does it matter now?" Aaron asked. Yet one look at Lisa let him know that wasn't the answer she was looking for.

When Lisa and Gina went to work the next day, the tabloid headlines confirmed the worst: PARIS FALLS TO THE

125

NAZIS—DE GAULLE FLEES TO ENGLAND. Lisa took Gina's hand and began to walk faster, almost in a march, until the two girls' strides were identical.

"We can make it, we can make it," they chanted, pushing the fear away.

At Platz & Sons, Lisa took her place at the machine, fastened her hairnet securely, and began another tiring day. She noticed that Mrs. McRae in front of her was wearing a black armband. At lunch her worst suspicions were confirmed.

"Did you hear?"

"Mr. McRae. Killed in Belgium he was, never made it to the beach for the boatlift."

"Just found out yesterday, she did. Can you believe she's come to work today?"

"That's what I'd do, if it were me."

The workers ate quickly, their lunch break had been cut to fifteen minutes. Lisa went back to work filled with awe for the British people, who didn't seem to cry, who sacrificed everything. She watched Mrs. McRae's hands tremble as the bowed figure in front of her sewed uniform after uniform.

"I'm very sorry to hear what has happened," Lisa said softly, leaning forward. Mrs. McRae took her hand and pressed it warmly, saying nothing, then lifted another pant leg onto her machine.

A button pinned to Mrs. McRae's lapel read "Support our men in arms."

The Fall of France left Britain alone to face Hitler, and the British steeled themselves for an expected invasion.

There was a growing sense of paranoia about enemy aliens in their midst. Women who were too blond were suddenly "suspect." A poster showing a sleek, sophisticated blond socialite surrounded by doting soldiers admonished: "Keep mum, she's not so dumb."

People were looking everywhere for spies. Workers of German and Austrian ancestry were laid off, and fifty thousand aliens were rounded up and put behind barbed wire in racetracks, at factories, and on distant islands like the Isle of Man.

It was long after lights out in the hostel when the whistle of the Grieg Piano Concerto in A Minor sounded insistently from the hallway outside Lisa's bedroom. She opened her eyes, leapt out of bed, and shook Gina. They dressed and rushed downstairs to the dining room, where Aaron and Paul stood in their pajamas, holding a candle.

"Gunter isn't back," Aaron said, worried.

It was only midnight; some of the other teenagers had been known to sneak in that late, but Gunter? He was never late; he was 100 percent dependable.

"What should we do?" asked Paul.

There was a noise down the hall and Hans appeared, tapping his hand on the wall for guidance. He slept in a cot off the kitchen, since it was decided that the third-floor dormitories would pose a hazard in a sudden evacuation.

"What's going on?" he asked.

"Gunter's missing. I think you should wake your mother."

"Me? Why me? I'm already blind, I don't want to lose my ears, too." They had all come to accept Hans's sarcastic brand of humor.

The group looked at Lisa, the meaning clear: She was the favorite, so it would fall to her to wake the matron.

She knocked gently on the door, but there was no response, so she had to rap as loudly as she could.

"What is it!" came the angry response.

"Gunter hasn't come home."

"Who?"

"Gunter's missing!" Lisa yelled through the door.

Mrs. Cohen appeared a minute later in the hallway, her long gray brown hair loose on her shoulders, not in its normal place on top of her head. She grabbed the telephone in the alcove and ran her finger down a list of telephone numbers on the wall.

"Is this the police station? This is Mrs. Cohen from the refugee hostel on Willesden Lane. I'm missing one of my charges."

Lisa watched as Mrs. Cohen's face darkened.

"Enemy alien! Is this a joke? He's a young boy," she shouted into the phone.

"I know he's sixteen, I know he's German . . . What do you mean he'll be interned! He's Jewish!"

Mrs. Cohen slammed down the phone and opened a thick handwritten book listing the names and addresses of each resident's employer. Finding the number of Mr. Steinberg, the man Gunter worked for, she dialed and explained the situation, then nodded in gratitude. "Thank you so much."

"Mr. Steinberg is English," she explained to the concerned teenagers. "He'll go right away to the police station and try to vouch for Gunter's loyalty. Now go to bed," Mrs. Cohen said.

They didn't. They lit more candles and sat around the dining room table and waited.

"Sixteen? Did Gunter have a birthday?" asked Paul.

"Last week. He didn't tell anybody but me," Gina said.

Aaron wandered into the dark living room and came back with the chess board. He set up the pieces and he and Hans played several games. The blind boy beat him almost every time.

"Let's make some tea," Lisa said.

"There is no tea," Gina reminded her.

"Let's get some mint leaves and boil some water," Lisa suggested, and the two girls took off toward the kitchen. There was an eerie light shining from the back of the house. They followed the flicker and were surprised to come across Johnny sitting on a milk crate, writing in his notebook by candlelight.

"Johnny! What are you doing?" Lisa asked.

"When I can't sleep, I write," he said nervously.

"May I see?" Lisa asked, leaning over to see, but Johnny put his huge hands over the page to cover it.

"Oh, no, no. It's not any good," he insisted.

"Would you like a mint tisane?" interrupted Gina.

"A what?" he asked.

"Tea, silly."

"No, thanks."

"Maybe you'll show me some other time," Lisa said, smiling, and headed out into the backyard.

"He's probably writing a love poem about you," Gina teased.

"Don't be ridiculous."

"I see the way he looks at you; it's the same way Aaron does."

"He does not!" Lisa said, brushing aside the comment, but in her heart she wondered if it was true.

At two in the morning, Hans and Aaron were still playing an endless endgame, chasing each other's king back and forth across the board. Lisa was bored silly.

"Hans," she said, "do you mind if I ask you something personal?" She tried to sugarcoat the question she had been wondering about for so long. "Have you always been blind?"

He made a chess move after feeling where Aaron had left his pawn, then let out a sigh, trying as hard as he could to sound flip. "No, God gave me this as his special present last year."

"Last year?"

"A mob at school beat me up the day after Kristallnacht. The actual diagnosis was that a chair leg hit my optic nerve. But not to worry, the Rabbi said it was a gift." His voice was dripping with sarcasm.

Lisa was stunned. "Why did he say that?"

"He said it was a gift because otherwise my mother would never have taken me out of Berlin. We'd still be there. She would never have left; she never thought it would happen to her." He paused for a breath, then went on. "You want to know a secret? She's never been to a synagogue."

The room was silent for a moment. Then Hans put his hands on the chess board again and made his move.

"Checkmate."

At three A.M. the committee adjourned and went to bed.

When Gunter finally came in late the following evening, he was surrounded by his friends. "Tell us what happened!" they said in unison.

Gunter had been on the double-decker bus coming back from Steinberg & Sons in the East End and looking out the window at the antiaircraft guns. His seatmate looked over, saw Gunter writing a letter in German, and called the police to arrest him as a spy. Gunter explained that he was writing a birthday card to the daughter of his employer and that he was Jewish; why would he be a spy? But he had a German accent and an alien registration card and was taken to the station.

Jewish or not, aliens over sixteen were being interned. Luckily, Mr. Steinberg showed up in time and signed an affidavit stating that Gunter's work at his factory was "critical to the war effort, and without him, the assembly line would shut down."

Lisa turned to Paul and Aaron with a worried look. "How old are you?"

"Fifteen," they replied in unison.

"But still, you better be careful."

When Lisa and Gina were getting up from the table, Johnny came and slipped Lisa a piece of paper, then left silently.

"See?" Gina said.

Lisa opened the envelope and read: "Please do not show this to anyone else." She turned away from Gina and unfolded a poem.

Always I see the faces
The faces at the station
The faces at the station
Are dimming before my eyes . . .

Always I hear the voices
The voices that are calling
That are calling out to me
But yet I cannot answer.

My mother, my father,
My sister, my brother
They are here now
Always
My heart is with them.

She looked up and saw Johnny staring at her from across the room. She was very moved by the simple words. Somehow his poem struck a chord in her heart in a way that was usually reserved for music alone. She winked at him and he smiled back, raising his pen as a salute.

She folded the paper neatly and put it in her pocket, safe from prying eyes.

14

*I*N THE SUMMER of 1940 the war came to the skies over Great Britain. Newspapers were awash in headlines of dog-fights between the Luftwaffe and the Royal Air Force; newspaper boys updated their chalkboards with daily tal-lies of how many Spitfires, Hurricanes, and Messerschmitts had been knocked out of the sky over the English Chan-nel. The coastline of southern England was first to be hit, as the Germans went after airfields and radar installations. Women of all ages fell in love with the image of the hand-some RAF pilot with his handlebar mustache, who flew scores of sorties on any given day, blasting the Jerrys out of the skies.

Lisa continued the difficult routine of factory work, pushing piece after piece of material through the sewing machine until her arms ached. Her mood picked up in the afternoon, as she counted the minutes left on the clock until her shift was over and she could get back to Willes-den Lane and her piano.

One afternoon, after a methodical search through the Cohens' sheet music, she chose Beethoven's beautiful *Pathétique* Sonata as her next goal. Professor Isseles had mentioned once that it was a "must-learn." She opened it and frowned in dismay.

"There's more black than white!" Aaron exclaimed, coming over to sit with her. "Looks like Beethoven spilled his inkpot all over the page," he said, looking at the thousands of black notes dotted close together on the page.

"No matter. I'll just start with the first one. Now move over!" She gave Aaron a flirtatious bump and he fell off the piano bench with a theatrical groan.

"Don't worry, Lisa, you can do it," came the reassuring voice of Hans from the nearby couch.

September 7 brought Lisa's disciplined routine to a halt. Saturday afternoon, as she was playing warm-up exercises, there came the piercing blast of the air raid siren. There had been many false alarms, so she kept playing. Why run to the shelter, as she had so often, and wait in boredom for nothing to happen? But then she heard the low rumble of approaching aircraft, and suddenly everyone came running down the stairs. Gunter grabbed Lisa by the arm and they raced onto the front lawn, training their eyes on the skies for a quick look, as the rest of the hostel ran by them into the convent, screaming.

"Hurry! It's for real! The Germans are coming!"

The *clack-clack* of the antiaircraft guns was the next indication that this was not the usual false alarm. The drone of the approaching bombers got louder and louder, then bursts of white smoke appeared high in the sky. Aaron was the last to watch before the matron yanked him by the sleeve and dragged him to the convent basement.

The London Blitz had begun.

The boys tried bravely to banter away their fear.

"That's a Jerry for sure, listen to the motor," Paul said as the noise got closer.

"No, that's ours, here it comes in for the kill!" Aaron answered.

Then no one could talk as the noise of the antiaircraft guns blasted their earsplitting barrage.

"That'll get 'em," one of the little boys bragged. But the next sounds were *boom, boom, boom*—each one a bomb, each one hitting their city of London. *Boom, boom,* and *boom* again; nothing the RAF or the antiaircraft guns could do stopped them. Lisa cowered in the corner under a blanket and held Gina's hand. The piercing sounds sent the horrible images of Kristallnacht racing again through her mind.

Several hours later, a short blast of the "all clear" sounded and residents from up and down Willesden Lane appeared in the streets, climbing out of basements and metal backyard shelters.

"We're all right, how about you folks?" came the nervous question echoing through the neighborhood.

"All okay here." "We're fine." "Us too," were the answers heard up and down the street.

Just as the neighbors began to collect themselves, someone yelled, "Look at the sky!"

Everyone looked up at the red glow. At first they thought it was a brilliant fall sunset. The red sky, however, was not in the west, it was in the east; the East End of London was burning.

After a brief respite the sirens sounded again and everyone descended once more into their protective shells and waited, terrified and confused.

Over the next forty-eight hours, they went back and forth, day and night, into the shelter. When the weekend was over, two thousand tons of bombs had been dropped onto the docks and industrial area of the Cockney heart of London—right in the neighborhood of Platz & Sons.

Monday morning, urged by the radio to go about their "normal lives," Gina and Lisa headed fearfully but patriotically to the underground train. When they came out of the station at Whitechapel, they were confronted by a confusion of hook-and-ladder brigades, civil defense workers, and families wheeling possessions in carts and baby strollers. The flames were mostly extinguished, but embers still smoldered, and the streets were littered with bricks. Chairs, tables, wardrobes, bureaus, and mattresses were being stacked in the streets as people pulled their possessions from the ruins. Housewives were sorting through soggy piles of clothing.

The corner shop where they'd bought penny candy had no window or door, but a hand-lettered sign had been stuck between two bricks: "Open for Business." A Union Jack dangled from the telephone wire.

Up ahead were piles of rubble. Gina stopped. "I think we should go back."

Lisa hesitated, looking around her in fear and dismay, but a housewife passed the two girls and waved. "A little bombing like this ain't gonna stop us, now, is it! We're going to work, aren't we!" She laughed as hard as she could, the white of her teeth flashing in bright contrast to the blackened soot covering her face.

"Yes! We're going to work!" Lisa shouted back, taking Gina's hand.

Continuing toward the factory, the girls dodged ladders and fire hoses and tried not to ruin their shoes.

Up ahead, two firemen were pumping water into a second-story bedroom. "Step back, please!" they yelled at the girls. "Wall's coming down, watch yourselves!" Wide-eyed, they looked on as the men yanked a cable and brought a whole precarious section of a damaged building tumbling down into a dusty pile of bricks.

"All right, girls, go on through, don't hurt those pretty feet!"

They picked their way through the bricks and arrived at Platz & Sons, which was mercifully intact except for a few broken windows. Mr. Platz himself was boarding them up. "Luvly day, good day, good morning, nice to see you," said the owner, greeting the workers at the door.

When Lisa sat at her station, she was amazed to see there wasn't a single empty seat. Everyone was at work, and the uniforms were flying off the assembly line in record time. Lisa felt tears of gratitude. These people weren't trembling under the Nazis the way she'd seen at home. They were gritting their teeth. If they could do it, so could she, she told herself, and for the first time in a long time, she felt some hope that Hitler might have met his match.

But Hitler seemed to have other ideas.

For a solid week the bombardment continued day and night, its fury concentrated on the shipping docks and ammunition dumps of the East End, and every night the residents of the hostel trudged into the shelter. On the mornings that followed, Lisa and Gina would head for work and emerge from the underground, never knowing which buildings would be in ruins and which would have been spared.

They learned to carry handkerchiefs to tie around their noses, to protect them from the acrid smoke of burning rubber and magnesium from the docks.

Sometimes the siren went off in the middle of the day and the workers had to rush into the basement of the factory. Mrs. McRae made it a point to grab Lisa's hand, pulling her down the stairs behind her. In spite of her terrible loss, Mrs. McRae used humor to help everyone through the worst. Hooking arms with the person in front, she hurtled down the stairs, singing:

"Here we go round the mulberry bush, the mulberry bush, the mulberry bush . . ."

It was silly, but it felt good to smile.

As the weeks went on, wave after wave of bombs continued their assault on the east side. In one terrible night alone there were a thousand fires. Workers began grumbling that their neighborhood was taking the beating for the whole country. But soon an errant bomb hit Buckingham Palace and the king and queen were photographed amid the damage. The grumbling turned to patriotism as people realized that even the royalty was taking its fair share.

Lisa and Gina and the other workers started leaving early so they could make the trip home before the sirens went off again. Lisa would run into the hostel and grab as many precious minutes on the piano as she could before another siren would blast.

One night, after an all-clear, they picked up leaflets that had fallen from the sky. "A Last Appeal to Reason," one read. The text was by Adolf Hitler and urged the English to give up before they were obliterated. Everyone laughed, but Lisa couldn't help wondering if the joke was on them.

When Britain gradually got the upper hand in the daytime, downing Nazi bomber after Nazi bomber, the Germans switched and bombed only at night. They had learned a costly lesson—this would not be the quick victory they had expected—for the first time since 1936, they couldn't roll in and over a country in a matter of weeks.

In a fit of patriotic fervor, Johnny announced that he had signed up for the "rescue squad." He showed off his metal helmet proudly, its large letter R painted across it.

"You're only fifteen, John," Mrs. Cohen said, chastising him.

"I wasn't asked my age, ma'am," he replied. "Only my weight," he added, provoking giggles from the group. Mrs. Cohen tried to look stern, but Lisa could tell she was as proud of him as everyone else was. Johnny was enormously strong, and God knew the rescue squad could use him. She went up and gave him a patriotic kiss.

The former precision of the hostel meal schedule was in shambles, for Mrs. Glazer never knew when the air raid siren would go off, forcing her into the shelter before she could finish her stews. Overdone cabbage and burned potatoes became a regular staple, but no one complained. In fact, complaining about anything seemed unpatriotic; one might as well be congratulating Hitler himself if you were caught moaning about the shortage of soap or toilet paper or sugar.

One night, huddled in the shelter, Lisa tried to figure out how she, too, could help the war effort. What could she do? She wasn't strong like Johnny. All she could do was play music. Suddenly it hit her; she could help raise morale by organizing a "musicale," a little concert of classical music and popular songs, and invite refugees from another hostel. The matron gave her approval; everyone was very excited. It gave them a sense of patriotic purpose.

Lisa asked for suggestions from Mrs. McRae about popular songs, and people at work donated sheet music. Her favorite was "Oh, Soldier, Who Is Your Lady Love?"

Hans agreed to play his favorite, which he had memorized from the BBC broadcasts, entitled, "When You're Up to Your Neck in Hot Water, Be Like the Kettle and Sing."

Gina wanted to help. "Let me sing the words."

"You can't sing," Lisa said without thinking.

"I can too. You just don't want anyone else to get any attention!"

Gina pouted for several days, until, realizing the program wouldn't be the same without her friend's enthusiasm, Lisa groveled and begged her to sing. They all stayed at the piano practicing until the last seconds of the now daily air raid blast, then had to be dragged by the matron into the shelter, still singing as loudly as they could.

The bombing continued mercilessly—no longer just in the East End but everywhere. The local town council inspected the hostel and announced that it was too risky having the boys' bedrooms on the vulnerable top floor, so the boys began sleeping in the living room and kitchen, where they were precious minutes closer to the bomb shelter.

Lisa understood the importance of this move but found it irritating nonetheless, since the younger boys liked to wrestle and chase each other through the living room and under the piano bench, disrupting her practice.

*   *   *

No one got much sleep. Every night the sirens sounded, and they would rush to the shelter for two or three hours, then stagger back to bed at the all clear. Some of the children chose to spend the whole night in the shelter, but the trade-off was waking up with frozen fingers and toes. When the bombing was at its worst, Johnny would be called and proudly joined the firemen in all-night stints. Lisa slept less and less and her face took on a drawn, worried look. Night after night she huddled in fear against the cold cement wall, praying for it to be over.

Hanukkah came, and Lisa was disappointed that once again Sonia was not allowed to visit.

Sonia had written her sister every week. The first letter had been almost unreadable, since it was written in English and Sonia hardly knew three words of her new language.

Lisa had responded in German, asking how everything was and telling her all the news of the hostel. But again the response had come in English, only slightly more intelligible than the last one.

When Lisa wrote back insisting that her sister write in their native tongue, she got a harsh reply.

"I promised to never more speak the words of Hitler," came the reply. Her fourteen-year-old sister was as stubborn as Lisa. Willpower seemed to be a family trait.

The musicale was scheduled for New Year's Day 1941. Mrs. Glazer had been hoarding butter so she could make mincemeat pies, and the other hostel forwarded two weeks' ration coupons for sugar. Gina was in good voice, only half joking that she was considering a singing career, and Gunter scrounged up a pair of castanets. Edith borrowed a neighbor's oboe and learned the five most relevant notes, while Johnny beat the time on his metal helmet.

It was only Aaron who didn't join in the festive mood. Lisa asked him to sit next to her as they practiced, but he refused.

"What's wrong, Aaron? Has something happened?" she asked.

"Everything has happened, look around you," he answered bitterly, going back to the sofa and staring at the chess board. Suddenly she noticed that the boy who had whistled the opening bars of the Grieg, founded the committee, and charmed her so was beginning to disappear into a cloud of angry solitude.

A week's lull in the bombing raised everyone's spirits and enabled the entertainers to put the finishing touches on their music program. But on December 29, the air raid siren sounded once again in the middle of evening practice. Everyone moaned and grabbed their books and the chess board and headed underneath the ground. Everyone but Lisa.

She was fed up with the horrible shelter. She needed to keep practicing! The bombs never hit anywhere near them, anyway, she told herself. There were no ammunition dumps in Willesden Green! She hammered the cascading octaves of the cadenza of the Grieg louder and louder to cover the whine of the bombers. Over and over she pounded the keys, and when the chords weren't loud enough, she began to shout the melody—drowning out the sound overhead.

The relentless explosions worked their way inside her head, and soon, without even realizing it, Lisa imagined herself single-handedly fighting a war against the Führer. Matching sound for sound in a pounding frenzy, she hurled chord after chord into the threatening skies, answering each explosion with one of her own. She played feverishly, her chords her only ammunition. She played with such intensity that she couldn't hear that the bombs were coming ever closer.

Suddenly there was a deafening crash, and the force of the bomb's concussion threw Lisa from the piano and smashed her against the living room wall. The glass of the bay window shattered and sent splinters showering across the room.

Lisa lay on the floor, wondering if she were dead. She looked at her hands first; the fingers moved, and so did the arms! She did a muscle-by-muscle inventory and discovered that everything worked. She was covered in dust and splinters but could discover no blood, so she stood up slowly. Instead of being terrified, she felt suddenly calm. These bombs can't hurt me! she told herself. She was fine; the piano was fine! The door flew open and Aaron and Gunter ran in.

"Lisa! Are you all right?" they yelled in unison.

"Just fine, you can tell Mr. Hitler I'm just fine!"

"I'll tell Mr. Hitler that you're crazy! Now let's go!" Aaron shouted angrily. She had never seen him so upset.

Another wave of airplanes was approaching; they each seized one of her arms, lifting her up and over the glass and back to the shelter.

Once underground, Mrs. Cohen grabbed Lisa, clasping her to her chest in relief. Releasing her, Mrs. Cohen scanned her charge from head to toe, making sure she was intact. Satisfied that Lisa was unharmed, she railed: "We are at war, young lady! It is not the time to take foolish risks. I had to send two boys to find you. You could have all been killed! Never, never do that again!"

Lisa apologized, too overcome to try to explain herself, and set about comforting the younger children. The raid lasted another six long hours. It was dawn when the neighborhood emerged from its shelters. The smell of smoke hung in the air with the dust and the fog. Four houses on the block, including the hostel, had been hit, and rescue crews were looking for the residents of 239. Their backyard had taken a direct hit and the shelter was covered with bricks and debris. Firemen were frantically digging them out. Everyone held their breath until finally the dusty man and wife appeared at the entrance and waved.

Willesden Lane cheered. They'd been lucky.

Lisa and Gina stood on the sidewalk, huddled under a blanket, and watched the firemen inspect the hostel. A hole was ripped through the roof, and the windows on the north side were completely blown out. When the firemen came out and gave the thumbs-up, Lisa joined a dozen others in rushing back into the building.

"Be careful, there's broken glass all around!" Mrs. Cohen yelled, but nothing she said could stop them.

Lisa had only one thought: Where were the photos of her mother and her father? She ran into her bedroom and found a layer of wet plaster covering her bed. Yanking open the drawer of the bureau, she pulled out their pictures, still intact, not even damp. She held them to her and read for the millionth time, *"Fon diene nicht fergesene mutter."*

What if she had lost them! She stared at her mother's downcast eyes. "I'm safe, Mama," she whispered, hoping to communicate across the distance to wherever her mother was. She wished so much she had news of her . . . where could she be? Would they ever let the letters through again? Please, dear God, let me have a letter, she prayed.

Mrs. Cohen pulled her from her thoughts by tugging

gently on her sleeve. "Please hurry, Lisa, pack your things, we have to go."

Mrs. Cohen helped pack the residents' suitcases and duffel bags, and the thirty-two children were led away by a civil defense captain to the community shelter to spend the night. They were officially homeless once again.

15

*N*O ONE knew exactly when the hostel would be habitable again. After the broken glass had been cleared from the front room, the residents were called back to the house for a brief meeting.

They finished cleaning out their drawers and were told to sit in the living room. Gunter, Aaron, and Johnny pushed the precious piano away from the cold air blowing through broken windows.

Mrs. Cohen addressed the morose assembly. "Quiet, please, for just a moment!" When the noise died down, she continued. "Mrs. Glazer and I have spent today contacting our neighbors and asking them if they could host you until our home is livable again. We have done our best to find you all homes as close by Willesden Lane as possible. Unfortunately, some of you will be placed outside of London temporarily. . . ."

A murmur of disquiet went through the group. "Please be patient, and bear with me!" The matron looked genuinely distraught at the prospect of sending the children away. "I know how important it is to all of you to remain in contact with each other; we've become a family. So you have my promise that I will do everything in my power to get our hostel repaired as soon as possible.

"Please wait until your name is called, then move as quickly as possible to the front door," continued the matron.

A line of families stretched from the front door out onto the sidewalk, waiting to pick up their charges.

"David Mittelman, Arnold Fogel . . . Gertie Sherman," the list began.

"Gina Kampf," Mrs. Cohen called, continuing to read from her hastily scribbled list. Gina stood up, hoisting her large suitcase, and waved forlornly at the committee. A nicely dressed woman put her arm around her and led her away. Lisa waved back at her sadly.

Lisa sat still for the next hour and watched her housemates and friends leave one by one. First Gina, then Gunter, then Aaron, her spirits sinking lower and lower as her friends left. Finally, Lisa's name was called; she was almost the last.

"Lisa Jura," Mrs. Cohen said finally, and the Quaker lady in black stepped into the foyer. Lisa looked up at her, surprised. This woman had done so much for her already!

"Hello, dear Lisa," said Mrs. Canfield. "Will thou forgive me for being so late? I'm so sorry, I wanted to get here early, but I was held up at meeting." She took Lisa's hand and helped her gather her belongings. Together they walked down the lane to Riffel Road.

Lisa paused shyly in front of her new home.

"Come in, please. Consider this house thine own," said Mrs. Canfield, as Lisa stepped into the foyer. The furnishings were austere; the chairs were wooden and the dining table very simple. There was none of the overstuffed comfort of the hostel living room—and there was no piano.

"I'm sure it is difficult being separated from your friends, but I will try to make thee a home nonetheless. We've all had a fright, now, haven't we," Mrs. Canfield said kindly, leading her up the stairs to a tiny bedroom. On the bureau was a framed photograph of a thoughtful-looking young man in a military uniform.

"That's my son, John. He's somewhere in Africa, I believe. He would be happy to know his room is being put to good use."

"He's very handsome," said Lisa, trying to make conversation.

"He's a medic," Mrs. Canfield said, looking at the photo lovingly. "We don't believe in fighting, of course, but he's doing his part to help his country. I'm very proud of him."

The next few months were agonizingly lonely. Each day Lisa would pass the empty hostel on her way to work and think of the friends and the piano she missed so desperately. After an arduous day at the factory, Lisa would return to the Riffel Road home and the two women would dine together, with little conversation passing between them. When the meal was over, they would sit in the parlor where Mrs. Canfield would read aloud from the Scriptures, Lisa taking whatever solace she could from the words.

The worst part, of course, continued to be the bombing raids; they had become less frequent, but now that their neighborhood had been hit, Lisa felt more vulnerable. The raids no longer came like clockwork every night, they were more erratic now, but not knowing when the next one would come made Lisa feel even less secure.

The air raid drill at Mrs. Canfield's was as follows: The siren blasted, and they rolled themselves out of warm beds, into their waiting shoes and coats, and out into the backyard. Mrs. Canfield carried a small lantern, which lit the way to the corrugated metal shelter that had been placed in the regulation three-foot-deep hole. It was freezing and damp, and week after week Lisa huddled on her cot and listened to the explosions while Mrs. Canfield snored gently.

When the explosions came close, Mrs. Canfield awoke and the two of them locked eyes during the agonizing seconds between the whistling sound and the boom. The longer the whistling lasted, it seemed, the louder and closer the explosion.

"Feel free to hum something, dear, it might make you feel better."

But Lisa's teeth were chattering too fast to allow her to carry a tune.

One night as Lisa lay in bed during a lull in the bombing, she heard a familiar whistling at her bedroom window. At first she thought she must be dreaming—but there it was again, the unmistakable melody of the Grieg piano concerto. Her heart leaped. She jumped up and saw Aaron at the window, trying to appear nonchalant, whistling as loudly as he could. She rapped on the window as an answer, then tiptoed through the house and opened the front door.

"Aaron!" she said excitedly.

"Hello, Miss Jura . . . lovely evening, isn't it? Care for a stroll?" he asked.

"I'll get my coat!" She ran back and bundled herself up,

paying careful attention in the mirror to the twist of her muffler.

They walked down Riffel Road to Willesden Lane and stood in front of the dark hostel. Lisa was aware of a shy distance between them. It had been nearly two months since she had seen him.

Aaron filled Lisa in on where he was living and how awful it was. He, too, felt isolated, and his host family was even more strict than Mrs. Cohen. Breaking off abruptly, he said, "Never mind all that . . . I want you to meet me tomorrow for lunch. I have a surprise for you."

"I only get fifteen minutes for lunch. You know that," she chastised him. "You're as irresponsible as ever." She made sure it sounded more like teasing than criticism.

"Just for an hour. You won't regret it."

"What is it that's so important?"

"It's a surprise. An important surprise."

She wanted to believe it was important, but in the back of her mind she didn't trust him. She couldn't afford to make her foreman angry; she was about to ask him for a change in assignment, since she was beginning to feel a lot of pain in her right hand.

"Trafalgar Square, at noon," he said commandingly.

But in a battle of wills, Lisa was usually the winner. "I refuse to come unless you tell me what it is."

"All right, it's two words."

"What?" she asked, agonizingly intrigued.

Aaron stopped for a second to prolong the suspense, then relented. "Myra Hess."

Lisa jumped for joy, throwing her arms around him.

*　　*　　*

She hated to lie to Mr. Dimble, but that's the way it had to be. She had thought of nothing else since Aaron had uttered the words *Myra Hess*. To think that she would finally see her idol!

"Mr. Dimble, I'm sorry, but I have to go somewhere at lunch today. I need an extra hour, please."

Mr. Dimble looked stricken; he pulled nervously at the pins stuck onto the felt sleeve protectors on his wrist. The factory was in full wartime schedule, and he lived and died by production targets.

"Today?"

"I have to renew my alien registration card," she fibbed, hoping he wouldn't know much about it. "I'll stay late and make up the time."

"Does it have to be today? Fridays are much easier," he said.

Lisa thought fast. "Tomorrow's my birthday, I have to do it before tomorrow."

"If it has to be, all right. I'll have someone cover your spot."

She ran up to the third floor to find Gina in the lunchroom and asked her to keep her secret. Then she flew out the door and into the tube station, which was, mercifully, not crowded—workers were sweeping out the mounds of debris that had been left behind from the previous night's use as an air raid shelter.

Trafalgar Square, by the north lion, he had said. It was so exciting. She looked up past the huge column in the center of the square and squinted at the sun for direction, but it was high noon and she couldn't tell which way was north, so she walked quickly 360 degrees around the square, gleefully disturbing the repose of scores of pigeons, until she saw Aaron. He was leaning on the huge bronze of the lion's ankle.

"Ready?"

"Ready!"

She grabbed his hand, overwhelmed by enthusiasm, running across the street and up the stairs of the imposing National Gallery. They joined a line of smartly dressed people who were dropping their shilling into a box in front of the sign: "Lunchtime Concerts at the Gallery—today's featured soloist, founder, Myra Hess." Gallantly, Aaron tossed in two shillings and they filed into the enormous foyer, where columns of serpentine marble stretched up to a giant domed ceiling. The gallery walls were bare; the paintings had been removed to protect them from the bombing—no one knew exactly where they had been taken, but rumor had it that Tintorettos and Vermeers were lining castle basements in Wales. A single Rembrandt canvas was on display, labeled "Picture of the Month."

The ornate architecture reminded her so much of Vienna, but she forced herself not to get melancholy and ruin this marvelous occasion.

A mammoth nine-foot grand piano was at the end of the gallery and hundreds of folding chairs were filling up fast with music lovers. She pulled Aaron by the hand and found the seat with the best visibility. Many of the elegant ladies wore extravagant hats; she had to take care not to sit behind one.

The program notes were written on a large chalkboard: Today's concert would be divided into two parts, the first, Miss Hess, solo piano, performing Bach's "Jesu, Joy of Man's Desiring," followed by Schumann's *Carnival*. The second half would be a Schumann string quartet.

A diminutive woman with short dark hair and a no-nonsense demeanor entered to a thunderous standing ovation and stood by the piano bench. "This performance is dedicated to the brave men and women who are serving Britain," she announced.

A shiver of pure exhilaration went through Lisa as the opening hush fell over the audience and the concert began.

The bell-like tone of the Steinway grand enveloped the large hall and filled Lisa's heart. What clear and heartfelt phrasing! What sure and steady fingers that could express the delicacy of the softest pianissimo without its tone disappearing. This was the way Professor Isseles had taught her to play—it was everything she was striving for in her music. Lisa allowed her mind to wander to the fantasy that had so often filled her in Vienna, of playing in front of a grand audience herself in a huge concert hall; she closed her eyes, and for an instant it seemed almost real. She lived a thousand dreams in the next forty minutes.

Aaron, seeing her expression, whispered, "What is it?"

"I used to hear her records in Vienna. . . . I can't believe I am really here!"

"Someday it will be you up there," he said, taking her hand.

Lisa smiled, but when she looked at her threadbare coat and worn shoes, she was overcome with the reality of her situation. How could a poor refugee girl ever make it to a concert stage? She didn't even have a piano to practice on anymore.

Lisa had been too wrapped up in the first part of the program to pay much attention to Aaron, but now that the string quartet had begun, she sneaked a look his way. He was handsome, she couldn't argue with that; she couldn't decide whether it was his long brown eyelashes or his rakish smile that she liked best. But suddenly, under the lashes, she noticed there were tears in his eyes.

She wished she knew more about him, but he had been so guarded about his past. She thought he had mentioned something about his father building bridges, but she couldn't quite remember.

Lisa hated when the beautiful notes slipped away and the concert ended. There was so much she wanted to say to Aaron. But now there was no time; she was needed back at the factory. She gave him a hurried thank-you hug and ran for the bus.

At lunch the next day she was embarrassed to hear Mrs. McRae and the other workers sing her a verse from "Happy Birthday." Gina began to laugh at Lisa's dismay but stopped when Lisa shot her a warning look. After blowing out the single candle on top of the tiny cupcake, Lisa split the sweet dessert with her as a payoff for her silence.

"I have some news," Gina said. "I'm not going to work here anymore."

"What do you mean? Why not?" Lisa asked, surprised and alarmed.

"The lady where I'm staying wants me to help take care of her new baby."

"Oh, no! How far away is it?" Lisa asked.

"Forty minutes by train. Not so bad, I guess."

Lisa felt suddenly abandoned.

"I won't just be a servant, though, like the last time," Gina said to cheer things up. "The lady says I can go to school in the morning! Isn't that wonderful?"

"Yes, it is," said Lisa, trying to hide her sadness as the buzz of the crowded lunchroom disappeared into the inner silence of another loss.

The whistle of the Grieg again sounded at her window that evening. Having hoped it would come again soon, she had laid out her shoes, her coat, and a muffler just in case. She tiptoed out the front door, leaving it slightly ajar.

She and Aaron strolled through the streets, darkened by the blackout, and once again the stars seemed to vibrate in the heavens. It was blessedly quiet; there were no antiaircraft guns or ambulances or air raids, though every few minutes a search beam would sweep the sky for enemy aircraft. They strolled slowly toward no destination in particular.

Aaron was as sweet and gentle as he had been the day before. She couldn't figure out what would make his moods so different one day to the next. Sometimes he'd be sarcastic and bitter, then gracious and sentimental, as he was now.

"Any news of the committee?" Aaron asked.

"Gina's got a new job as a nanny."

"I wonder how long that'll last?" He laughed. "Oh, did you hear about Paul?"

"No, is he all right?"

"They picked him up the day after he turned sixteen. He's on the Isle of Man."

"That's terrible, how could they? It's so stupid."

"It's so British."

"That's mean."

"But don't worry, Gunter got a letter from him. He says he's fine and that the food is better than it was at the hostel. Says there are lots of Nazis and spies but they don't say much or they'll get beaten up. In six months they're going to let him enlist in the army."

They kept walking and passed the entrance to the tube station at Willesden Green. A family with small bundles was going in for the night. The deep underground stations were favorite bomb shelters, and some people preferred to spend the night on the platforms even when the sirens hadn't gone off, just in case.

"Aaron, I want to ask you something personal, please don't be angry," Lisa began.

Aaron didn't say anything, so Lisa continued.

"What were you crying about yesterday at the concert?" She had been reliving this moment for the last two days.

"I wasn't crying," Aaron said.

Lisa had expected as much, but she didn't stop. "Please tell me?"

"Memories. That's all, just memories."

"Bad memories?"

Aaron was silent for a moment. Lisa didn't interfere.

"Good memories, they're the worst kind."

"About your family?"

Aaron nodded.

"You've never even told me where you were from."

"Mannheim. On the Rhine."

She was quiet, hoping he would go on.

"I was remembering the chamber music at our house," he said finally.

"You had chamber music at your house?" she said, surprised.

"When I was younger I used to fight with my mother about having to go downstairs and listen—all I wanted to do was stay in my room and build bridges, like my father did. I had hundreds of metal strips and screws and bolts that my father had made for me. . . ." His voice drifted off for a moment, then started up again. "Sunday nights, though, they made me listen to chamber music in the salon. Actually I liked it; it was quite good, you would have loved it."

"But why were you crying?" she asked gently.

"It's what happened when the chamber music stopped. My father was very influential in Mannheim, you see, just like his father and his father's father. He had designed the major new bridge over the Rhine. The members of the philharmonic came to the house, so did the mayor. I mean, they used to come before they were told not to—by the Nazis." They kept walking. Aaron disappeared for a while into the memory of his story.

"And then?" Lisa asked, prodding gently.

"Then nobody came to the house anymore. And they closed my father's office; he had to stay home all the time. One Sunday night, he dressed up again in his black tie, opened the front door and waited for the guests to arrive. My mother was crying as she watched him waiting and waiting. Of course, nobody came."

Lisa waited as Aaron exhaled a huge sigh and then continued. "Then he walked out the door . . ."

Lisa waited for Aaron to go on, but he didn't.

"Then what happened?"

"They found him floating in the river . . . near the bridge he had built."

Lisa started to cry and he took her hand. They walked quietly through the streets, treasuring the comfort of each other's presence. At the corner, in the dark under the streetlight, he put his arm around her and kissed her. She felt her heart beginning to give way.

16

*I*N THE SPRING of 1941 the crocuses came up in strange places; they poked their leaves between sandbags, from under piles of bricks, from anywhere their corms had been blasted by the force of the bombs.

At 243 Willesden Lane they came up in the front yard and were a welcome mat of purple flowers for the reopening of the hostel.

Repairs had been expedited at the insistence of Mrs. Cohen, who wanted her charges to be reunited as soon as possible.

She and Hans and Mrs. Glazer had lived in the house during that period, and Hans later told Lisa that his mother had admitted to feeling lonely without the chaos.

The day the children were to return, she had made sure that the postponed gingerbread cookies were finally baked and that as much meat as possible was procured from her network of donors, do-gooders, and neighborhood shopkeepers.

Lisa prepared to move. As she rolled up her scarves and folded her pleated skirts, she looked around the bare room with a nostalgic feeling. The weeks had gone by faster than expected, and she had come to honor Mrs. Canfield's steady kindness and support. She had learned a little about the "Friends" and their belief in pacifism. One thing made her admire them especially. Mrs. Canfield told her about letters she had received from Quaker friends in Germany, who in response to the Nazi greeting *"Heil Hitler"* would say, *"Grüss Gott,"* meaning "Hello" or "Good day." Many had been jailed because of their insolence.

Mrs. Canfield had also helped Lisa with her English— every night for fifteen minutes without fail. It wasn't quite as good as a real school, but it was learning, and Lisa was hungry for it.

On the day of the move, Mrs. Canfield escorted Lisa around the corner to the hostel, embracing her as they said good-bye.

"I promise I'll come visit," Lisa said.

"That would make me very happy. I hope thou knowest how comforting it was to have thee—it helped me so with my worries about John so far away. My house will always be thy house."

Mrs. Cohen greeted each child with a smile and a hug; there was a softness in her that had replaced her former aloof demeanor. She had missed them.

Lisa walked happily in the front door and immediately noticed the changes. The blackout curtains now had draw-strings and could be rolled up in the daytime—making it much more bright and cheerful. The windows were clean, the carpet spotless, and Mrs. Cohen's Victrola was now in the place of honor in the recess of the bay windows—the place where the piano had been and where it was no longer.

Lisa was stunned. Had the piano been damaged? Had Mrs. Cohen been angry and taken it away? Lisa saw Mrs. Cohen glancing at her nervously.

Suddenly, a group of teenagers led by Johnny, Aaron, and Gunter jumped out from the hall and yelled, "Surprise!"

Lisa was now totally confused. Before she could remind them that it wasn't her birthday, her friends circled around her, pushing her down the hall into the kitchen. The cellar door was standing open.

"Follow me, Maestro," said Johnny, turning on the light.

Lisa followed him down the stairs into the moldy basement. The pickles and preserves had been moved—in their place was the sturdy old upright piano.

Mrs. Cohen stepped carefully down two stairs from the top and peered into the room: "It's not the Royal Albert Hall, but if you insist on playing through the bombings, at least you should play where it's safe."

Lisa was speechless. When she recovered her manners she turned around and said, "I don't know how to thank you."

"You should thank them," Mrs. Cohen said, pointing to Johnny, Aaron, and Gunter. "They did all the work." The boys took a bow. "Now, be sure you practice! I would hate to think they brought such a heavy load down these stairs for nothing!"

Lisa kissed Johnny and Gunter, then gave a romantic smooch to Aaron and the room broke out in whistles. The younger boys poked their heads in from the kitchen door, adding "Play something, Lisa!"

Everyone crowded around the piano, pushing aside tins

of peas and carrots and cleaning supplies to get a better look.

Lisa decided on something playful and romantic, an Impromptu of Schubert. She hadn't played in a while, and she was nervous at first. She stretched her fingers, shaking them out above the keys, then launched into the piece.

One of the eleven-year-olds blurted out: "Go, Lisa!"

"V for Victory!" another added, and everyone laughed.

After the first few chords, Lisa called out loudly up the stairs, "Oh, Mrs. Cohen! You had the piano tuned! Thank you so much!" Mrs. Cohen beamed back; Lisa could only imagine how complicated it must have been, with the rationing and the lack of money and the million other repairs that the matron was responsible for. She finished the short Schubert piece with a flourish and everyone clapped. Looking around at the familiar faces, she realized how deeply she had missed her Willesden Lane family.

"All right, no more time for fooling around, everyone! I have posted the chore lists, so let's get to work!" the matron said forcefully, and the teenagers boisterously pushed each other up the stairs, happy to be shoving and joking and tripping over their friends again.

Mrs. Cohen came over to Lisa as she was closing the piano. "Miss Jura? Please come to my room before dinner, I want to talk with you about something."

"Yes, ma'am," Lisa said nervously, worried as always by the formal tone of the matron's voice. Had she done anything wrong? Maybe she shouldn't have kissed Aaron in front of everyone.

The children of Willesden Lane reinstalled themselves in their bedrooms and quickly discovered that the house wasn't repaired as completely as it first appeared. Sheets of plastic still covered part of the roof, one of the boys' dormitories had plywood in the window frames, and several unlucky boys had to bunk in the hall. Makeshift boards covered a hole in the floor of the boys' bathroom. It took no time at all for some of the younger boys to realize they now had a wonderful view directly into the girls' bathroom. They took full advantage until the girls caught on and pelted them through the hole with wet towels.

Lisa opened her suitcase and started to unpack, looking over sadly at Gina's empty bunk. She heard a crashing from the stairs, and Aaron, breaking the rules, careened into the girls' dormitory, followed shyly by Gunter.

"Hey, you've got windows!" he said, tapping on the new panes of glass, then went over and lay back on Gina's empty bed. "Gina's lazy, that's what I think."

"I thought at least she'd come by and say hello," Gunter added. "She knew we were all coming back today."

"You ought to go visit her, Gunter," said Lisa. "Go visit and tell her to come back."

"She won't. If she comes back, she'll have to go to work again," Aaron said. "She's lazy!"

"She is not!" Gunter protested halfheartedly.

"We know you're sweet on her, so don't pretend," Lisa said, teasing.

Gunter exhaled in frustration, then got up and went downstairs. Lisa smiled at Aaron, who took her arm and escorted her downstairs to the dining room.

"Save me a seat, I have to talk to Mrs. Cohen," Lisa said, giving him a playful push.

Lisa prayed the meeting with Mrs. Cohen would have something to do with her music—and not be any bad news about the many things she always worried about—her parents, Rosie, and Sonia. She knocked on the door nervously.

"Come in, please," the matron said.

The room had been rearranged since the bombing and all the breakable clutter had been removed, making it as sparse as the Quaker house. Mrs. Cohen was sitting on the bed; in front of her was an open copy of the *Evening Standard* newspaper.

"I've been saving this to show you," Mrs. Cohen said, pointing to a small announcement in the middle of the page.

It read: "Auditions for scholarships at the Royal Academy of Music. Applications being accepted through April 1. Open to all students with a proficiency in musical performance of the classical repertoire."

The London Royal Academy? Lisa felt a rush of emotion. This was where the great musicians studied; this was where Myra Hess herself had studied! Could she possibly qualify for such a school?

"Would you like to apply for an audition?" Mrs. Cohen asked.

"Would they let a refugee girl go to the Royal Academy?" Lisa asked incredulously.

"Why shouldn't they? There's no shame in being a refugee, young lady," Mrs. Cohen scolded.

Lisa was overwhelmed, not just with the possibility of an audition, but with gratitude toward the matron. She could hardly believe that someone was actually looking out for her, helping her with decisions about her future. She was so used to having only herself to rely on since she'd said good-bye to her parents two years ago.

"But I haven't studied in three years."

"You've been practicing, haven't you?"

"I haven't had a teacher, maybe it's all been wrong," she said, suddenly feeling terribly insecure.

"Don't you trust your ability, dear?"

Lisa's eyes were shining, but she was tongue-tied.

"I take it you do. Are you interested?"

The phrase "make something of yourself" had never been far from her consciousness, and now it was center stage in her mind. She knew this would make her mother so proud. It would be the first thing she would tell her when she saw her. An audition at the Royal Academy!

"Yes, ma'am. I am," she answered firmly.

"Good. Now, let's go to dinner."

Mrs. Glazer carried out the steaming platters of meat, and the crowded table clapped in appreciation. She paused before rushing back to the kitchen and said: "It's so nice to have all of you back again. If truth be told, I missed your mess, it's been downright boring without you!" Everyone laughed.

When it was time for the lighting of the candles, everyone noticed that it was Mrs. Cohen who, for the first time, uttered the blessing. She was seated beside the rabbi from the neighborhood synagogue. She tapped her fork on the wine glass.

"Rabbi Silverstein spoke to me today about how important it is for all of us to have faith . . . to keep on with our lives. I know these months have been difficult for you away from our home here on Willesden Lane . . . but I'm also aware that the months in front of us will perhaps be even more trying. Many of you have shared with me your tremendous worries for the safety of your families and loved ones on the continent . . ." Uncharacteristically, her voice choked, and she motioned to the rabbi seated next to her.

He stood and cleared his throat. "I wish I had some concrete news to report. As you no doubt have heard on the radio, Hitler is trying to frighten us with threats on the very future of the Jewish people. It is a time that tests our faith to the limits of our endurance, and we must all join forces and pray together to help one another survive through these terrible moments. Please join me in thanks for the warmth and friendship that surrounds you here."

There was total silence at the table. The rabbi looked at the young faces, made too serious and too adult before their time. "I look forward to seeing you all tomorrow at synagogue," he said, standing to leave.

Mrs. Cohen held up a small pile of correspondence. "Not many letters are getting through, I'm afraid, but I do have a few . . . Lewin, Kingman, Weisel, Jura, and Mueller."

The letters were passed down the line to waiting hands, and Lisa took hers gingerly. The stamp had the words *República de Mexico* engraved on it and she didn't recognize the name on the return address. She quickly stuffed it in her pocket.

"Aren't you going to read it?" Aaron asked.

"It's not polite, I'll wait until after dinner," she bluffed. But the truth was that Lisa was always terrified when she received a letter. The only thing worse than getting a letter was not getting one. The news was never good and brought so many disappointments. She resolved to enjoy what was left of the Sabbath dinner before learning what worrisome things awaited her. She would read it and cry herself to sleep later.

*   *   *

After the *Kinder* devoured dessert, they got up from the table with an enormous scraping of chairs and headed for the social pursuits of the living room. Mrs. Cohen must have known her Victrola would be wildly popular. The one rule she had set was that Hans was the only one allowed to touch the fragile 78 rpm records. He took them meticulously from their envelopes and placed them by feel onto the platter, as trustworthy Edith dropped the needle and the room was filled with sound.

But Lisa wasn't interested; the letter was burning a hole in her pocket.

"Get your coat, let's go next door," Aaron whispered in her ear. She nodded and disappeared upstairs.

The convent door was open. Aaron had brought a blanket and a candle, and they made themselves comfortable in one of the rooms in the front of the building.

"Will you read it to me?" Lisa asked in a small, frightened voice, handing him the letter. She was grateful to be in his presence, no longer confined to the solitude she had felt before when reading letters.

He opened the envelope with care; the blue airmail paper was covered with neat handwriting and dated March 20, 1941, only the week before.

"Dear Lisa, My name is Alex Bronson. I am your brother-in-law Leo's cousin. I am writing you to see if you have any information regarding Leo and Rosie, as we have lost contact with them since their escape to Paris."

"Paris? They made it to Paris?" Lisa asked, relieved and worried at the same time.

Aaron continued reading: "In case you haven't heard, Rosie and Leo pretended to be drunken Dutch tourists returning after a New Year's Eve in Vienna and successfully fooled the Nazi guards into letting them get on the train.

They traveled to Antwerp, where my father helped smuggle them to France. We got a postcard a month later saying that they'd gotten married, then our visas came through and we left for Mexico. That was eight months ago and we have had no news of them since."

Lisa let out a sob. She remembered the terrible vision she had seen in the newspaper of Hitler strutting under the Arc de Triomphe in Paris.

Aaron handed her his handkerchief and waited until she calmed down.

Lisa finally nodded. "Go on."

"We pray Leo and Rosie have been able to leave France because we are receiving news that Jews are no longer safe there; deportations have begun to camps in Poland. We are making inquiries to the Red Cross but have gotten nowhere. We are hoping that you may have received some word of them and could get in contact with us, since they do not have our address in Mexico."

Lisa shivered as she thought about her beautiful sister and tried to conjure up an image of her and Leo safe somewhere. Were they hiding somewhere? Had they escaped?

Her head kept spinning.

Her thoughts were interrupted by the air raid siren sending out its shrill call. Aaron and Lisa waited in each other's arms until they saw the procession of lanterns and footsteps from next door, heading for the convent.

"Be careful, Johnny," they heard Mrs. Cohen say outside as she said good-bye to the brave volunteer who headed off to fight the fires that were sure to come somewhere in the next few hours. They then joined the parade to the bomb shelter beneath them, to wait out the terror of another night.

The raid was mercifully short. Maybe it was the comfort

of the Willesden Lane reunion that buoyed Lisa's spirit, or the hours spent in Aaron's arms. Whatever it was, Lisa was humming the Grieg concerto to herself when the all clear signal sounded and the *Kinder* tramped upstairs to a blissful sleep.

17

$\mathcal{T}$HE NEXT DAY, as soon as the dishes from breakfast were washed and the last person helped out the front door, Mrs. Cohen went to the telephone in the alcove and called Bloomsbury House. Mr. Hardesty took her call immediately.

"Good morning, Mrs. Cohen, I trust the first night back went well?"

The matron sped through the small talk and got right to the subject of Lisa's audition. "Are there any funds available to help with the ten pounds necessary for the application fee?" she asked bluntly.

"I hope you won't take this the wrong way, Mrs. Cohen, but the Royal Academy is a very prestigious school. Just getting accepted is difficult enough, but a scholarship?"

"Surely there must be some cultural fund, it's just ten pounds," Mrs. Cohen persisted.

"I am sorry, Mrs. Cohen, but whatever funds we have

available for cultural matters should be put to use for all the children . . . on things that aren't so, ah, improbable."

"Improbable?" she asked icily.

"I know Miss Jura is a lovely young lady, and I am sure that she plays beautifully, but—"

"Mr. Hardesty, I know you have a very busy schedule, but I'd like you to come to the hostel tomorrow at five o'clock."

There was silence and the hint of an exasperated sigh on the other end of the line.

Mrs. Cohen continued: "Perhaps if tomorrow isn't convenient, the next day would—"

"I'll be there tomorrow, Mrs. Cohen."

"Thank you very much," she said, and hung up smiling.

At the factory, Lisa was in an exuberant mood as her overactive imagination spun tales of fame and glory. It was much too early to mention anything to anyone about this faint, almost minuscule hope of an audition, but that didn't stop her from thinking about it every living second.

Mrs. McRae noticed Lisa humming—not a sentimental love song like those other young ladies hummed when they worked, but funny-sounding la, la, ti, das. "Got a new beau, dear?" she asked.

Lisa remained mysterious. She just winked and kept humming.

Mrs. McRae laughed. "You're an odd duck," she said, and returned to her work.

At four o'clock sharp Lisa ran out the door and caught the underground train home; she couldn't wait to start practicing.

Mrs. Cohen intercepted her on the way down the stairs to the basement. "Lisa?"

"Yes, ma'am?"

"I wonder if you'd mind playing the Grieg concerto for us. You do that so well. If you leave the door open, we can hear it up in the kitchen."

Lisa agreed, flattered by the attention.

At five o'clock to the minute, Mr. Hardesty rang the bell and Mrs. Cohen welcomed him with a finger to her lips and a gesture, guiding him to the back of the house.

She asked him to stand at the top of the cellar stairs, where he listened to the thunderous cascading octaves of the cadenza of the Grieg Piano Concerto in A Minor. No upright piano Mr. Hardesty had ever heard had sounded like this. He could hardly believe he wasn't in a concert hall. He tiptoed closer, descending the rickety steps one by one. He watched as Lisa's hands traveled over the keyboard with astounding speed and dexterity.

Lisa's concentration never broke; she never even noticed his presence. Ten minutes later, he came back up the stairs into the kitchen.

"I had no idea," he said to Mrs. Cohen, fishing into his pocket for his worn leather wallet. "I'd be honored to pay for the fee myself," he said, handing her a ten-pound note.

Mrs. Cohen couldn't hide a knowing grin, but she thanked him politely as she pocketed the money.

At the factory, Lisa decided it was time to include Mr. Dimble and Mrs. McRae in her "other life," and she asked if she could work a shorter shift (with a cut in pay, of course) to allow extra time to practice. She showed them the newspaper clipping with its impressive "Royal Academy" logo and told them of her plans to apply for an audition.

"My, my, that's very posh," Mr. Dimble said, somewhat skeptical.

"Have a heart, Raymond, you've let other people have shorter shifts before, I've seen you! Why not let her off to practice the piano?" interjected Mrs. McRae.

Mr. Dimble shook his head as though it were way beyond his understanding.

"Three o'clock it is, then, but no slacking off before then, my girl!"

"Thank you so much," Lisa called after him as he headed down the line to intercept a cartload of fabric.

Mrs. McRae turned back once more. "Very exciting, all this. You'll 'ave to come over and play for us East Enders sometime. There's a piano at the pub," she said quickly before immersing her head back in her work.

"I'd love to," Lisa promised, eyes shining.

After work, Lisa went straight to the Royal Academy of Music in the heart of London. She hadn't been to the city center since the devastation of the December firebombs and was disheartened to see the tremendous destruction. Whole blocks were burned to the ground; the House of Commons was badly damaged; churches and taverns were in ruins. Luckily, St. Paul's Cathedral had escaped. Johnny had told her about the all-night fire brigades that had saved the great church.

In the midst of the bombed-out buildings, men with pin-striped suits and umbrellas were walking energetically around roadblocks as if nothing at all were strange.

The Royal Academy had also escaped damage. Lisa approached the five-story brick building with a pounding heart and climbed the exterior staircase with its majestic canopy of glass and wrought iron and entered the large foyer, which was presided over by gilded portraits of King Edward and Queen Elizabeth. A magnificent spiral staircase wove upward five floors to a dome above her head. The sounds of French horns, bassoons, and violins descended into a booming cacophony around her.

Even though she realized it was probably bad luck, Lisa couldn't help but fantasize about what it would be like to study in this exalted institution, following in the tradition of so many of the greats.

She had been worried about how she was dressed, but the serious students who strode by were too busy to notice her at all. She quickly located a sign that led her to the registrar's office.

The secretary was polite and reached behind her for a packet of papers, handing the mimeographed sheets to Lisa. "The deadline for the application is next Friday. Please fill out your choice of repertoire and bring the completed form back to us."

As she walked out, Lisa again studied the young men and women who were rushing by her, carrying music cases and smoking cigarettes. She heard snatches of their conversations, which included words like "art" and "soul" and "beauty." It was all too wonderful.

Arriving home, Lisa ran to find Hans. "I've got the application, come sit with me, so we can go over it."

They got right to work, Hans sitting cross-legged on the sofa as she read: "Applicants are advised to carefully select repertoire to display to best advantage the full range of their capabilities."

"This is so fantastic!" he said, interrupting her, as excited as if it were his own audition.

"All repertoire must be performed by memory," she continued. "Well, of course!"

"That's obvious," Hans echoed. "Now . . . what are you going to play?"

Lisa continued reading: "The applicant will be required to perform a work from each of the major stylistic periods in classical literature. First: Bach—choose a prelude or fugue from the *Well-Tempered Clavier*." Lisa thought for a second, then shouted: "The D Minor!"

"Not a bad idea," Hans agreed. "All right, next."

"A sonata by Beethoven," she read. "I could do the Thirty-two Variations!"

"It said a sonata," Hans corrected her.

"Oh, I did the early A Major when I was in Vienna," she offered, and hummed the opening phrase.

"Not strong enough. Don't forget the competition is going to be tough, you have to amaze them. What about the *Pathétique?*"

"I only just started it."

"Then do you know the *Waldstein?*"

"Heavens, no! I'd rather do the *Pathétique!*"

"The *Pathéthique* it is, then," Hans said firmly.

Lisa kept reading: "A major work by a romantic composer: Chopin, Schumann, Schubert, Brahms . . . That's simple, I'll do the Chopin nocturne, the one that you like."

"Not substantial enough."

"But I'm really good at it!" Lisa said defiantly.

"Not possible." Hans lost himself in thought for a moment. "I know just the piece. It was written for you." He got up, felt his way to the Victrola, and turned it on to warm up. He pointed to the stack of records.

"Find me the Rubinstein recording. I want you to hear Chopin's Ballade in G Minor."

Obediently she found it and guided the needle into

place. They lay back on the sofa and listened to the heart-breaking and passionate ballade. It was Romanticism incarnate.

"It's everything that you are, Lisa. You must play it," Hans commanded.

They listened as Rubinstein furiously attacked the difficult and thunderous chords of the coda. It sounded as if all hell were breaking loose on the keyboard.

"Do you think I can do that?" Lisa's eyes were wide in amazement.

Hans looked momentarily worried. "I forgot about the coda. Do you think it's too difficult?"

The very words *too difficult* sparked Lisa's competitive spirit. Wasn't she Lisa Jura, the prodigy of Franzenbrückestrasse, the one who made all the neighbors proud? What would Mama say if she missed her chance because a piece was "too difficult"? She listened to the roiling passion in Rubinstein's notes, nodded to herself, and said simply, "Yes, this is the piece."

From the moment she found the sheet music to the Chopin ballade in a second-hand music store, it seemed to everyone on Willesden Lane that Lisa never stopped practicing.

She practiced from four to six in the afternoon, ate dinner, then continued from eight to nine. She had just under a year until the audition date, and she knew she'd need every moment to learn two major new works. Aaron would often come down to the cellar, give her words of encouragement, then slip out of the hostel to go about his business.

Hans was her mainstay. He became expert at feeling his way down the wooden stairs and sat quietly in a chair next

175

to the piano, reading his braille textbooks. His was a comforting presence. Lisa marveled at how he had changed in the year since his arrival at the hostel. He had toned down the sarcasm about his blindness, perhaps accepting it more, or perhaps realizing that no one was laughing at his blind man jokes. These were terrible times for everybody, and sometimes sympathy was in short supply.

Lisa wondered what it must be like for Hans to lose his sight after having been able to see for his first fourteen years. She closed her eyes as she played and tried to imagine never being able to see again, but she couldn't stand it for long and had to open them again. At moments like this she wanted to throw her arms around her new friend, but she knew that would injure his considerable pride, so she settled for a simple "Hello over there, Hans, it's so nice to have you keep me company." His smile was a rich reward.

She went about learning the notes in a methodical way, and day by day, she started getting the feel of the Chopin and Beethoven pieces into her hands.

Her favorite break from practicing came after dinner, when she, Aaron, Gunter, and Hans got their turn at the record player. Mrs. Cohen had imposed strict rationing of Victrola time after fights had broken out about the choice of music. Edith had been playing the same Benny Goodman record so often that there was now a large annoying scratch, which made the music skip every few seconds.

"Maybe I should break the blasted record," Aaron offered in all seriousness.

"Aaron!" Lisa chastised. "Don't you dare."

Johnny's favorite record was by Glenn Miller. After

working his twenty-four-hour shift at the fire station, he cherished his twenty-four hours off at the hostel, when he would wait for the trombone solo and lift his head for a few minutes from the papers in front of him. The rest of the time he scribbled endlessly in his notebooks. Occasionally he showed a poem to Lisa, who thought them deeply evocative. She called him her fellow "artiste."

While Johnny was not a part of the committee itself, its members had come to appreciate him. The younger children had adored him all along; they loved to sit on his huge shoes and have him lift them up with his legs as he continued to write in his notebook all the while. Ever since Lisa had said how much she liked his poems, he had become more accepted by her friends. She encouraged him to share his work with the rest, but he resisted, saving his poetry for Lisa alone and showing the others only his affable goodwill and occasional goofy antics to the rhythm of Glenn Miller's jazz.

When it was time for Lisa's turn at the Victrola, she and Aaron listened for the millionth time to Arthur Rubinstein's recording of Chopin's ballade, as she laid her head against his shoulder. They lay close to the funnel shaped speaker, trying to filter out the noise of the children playing around them. If they were lucky, there would be no air raid siren, and they could spend a magical thirty minutes floating in the beauty of music.

Lisa listened carefully to every nuance. But listening to a recording wasn't the same as having a teacher. Hans helped the best he could, but it was difficult to untangle the complicated fingerings she needed to maximize her power and finesse.

If only Professor Isseles could be here to help, she thought. Yet it wasn't really the professor she yearned for, it was her mother. Some nights she would put her head on the keyboard and cry, "Mama, why can't you be here to help me?" She missed her desperately.

Victrola time in the living room was difficult for Gunter. It was summer already and he had seen Gina only once since everyone had moved back to the hostel and he was looking more and more like a lost puppy.

One Saturday afternoon Aaron arrived with a package under his arm. He whispered for Lisa to join him in the presentation. He handed it to Gunter and made him open it. It was a pair of ladies' silk stockings.

Lisa gasped in amazement. "Aaron! Where did you get these?"

Silk stockings were an unimaginable luxury during the war, strict clothes rationing had made them impossible to find. Silk was for parachutes, not for stockings.

"Why are you giving Gunter silk stockings? I'm the one who needs them!" Lisa demanded with more than a hint of jealousy.

"Dum, dum, da dum dum," Aaron whistled. "I have a mission for the committee. Poor Gunter is so down in the dumps, he's no fun anymore. We're going to go visit Gina and give her these. After that, I have an even bigger surprise!"

Remembering the magic of the Myra Hess concert—Aaron's last surprise—Lisa softened.

"When are we going?"

"Tomorrow."

The next day, Lisa felt guilty about missing her practice session but allowed Aaron to talk her into it. Besides, she was feeling a little more tired each day and told herself that maybe a little time off would rest the aching muscles in her arms.

The threesome hurried to the train station. Aaron paid for everybody's fare, which Lisa thought extravagant.

"Did you get a promotion or something?" she asked.

"Maybe yes, maybe no," he answered, cryptically.

"Ooh, you can be so annoying," she said, but took his hand and smiled. It was no time for a fight.

Lisa didn't push him—she was used to his behavior by now. Aaron never spoke about his work; the little she knew about his job (as a machinist grinding valves for army trucks) came from Gunter. Aaron always found a charming way of brushing aside her questions.

Richmond was a wealthy suburb of London south of the Thames. Richmond Park had its own herd of tiny deer and acres of fancy rhododendrons. German bombers hadn't been interested in this part of town, and the streets were as clean as they were idyllic, with houses that were much like what Gina had been used to in her previous life in Vienna.

Finding 25 Temple Hill Road was more difficult than they had anticipated, since all the street signs had been removed at major intersections. The three friends went round and round the same block.

At one point in the confusion, Lisa realized they were yelling at one another in German. "Shhhhhhhh!" she said, panicky. "They'll think we're spies and shoot us!" The others quieted down immediately, realizing that as ridiculous as it might seem, it could easily happen.

Finally, they located the house and knocked. A uniformed butler came to the door.

"Is Gina Kampf at home?" Aaron asked.

The butler looked at the teenagers and cleared his throat. "She didn't say she was expecting visitors. . . ."

Aaron moved forward. "Please tell her the committee has arrived with her tickets," he said grandly.

The butler looked at them skeptically, but good manners won out. "Just one moment," he said, and disappeared behind the heavy mahogany door.

Lisa started to giggle. "What tickets?"

"Just wait," he said, reaching in his pocket for a mysterious envelope and waving it before her eyes.

Gina's mouth dropped when she saw her friends standing on the doorstep.

Gunter stepped forward. "I've brought you a present," he said proudly, and handed her the package.

Gina shut the front door behind her, sat on the porch steps, and opened her present. She held up the stockings, amazed. "Ooh! Thank you so much!" she cried, delighted. She kissed Gunter on the cheek, and he blushed a deep red.

"You're w-welcome," he stammered, trying to regain composure. Gina saw his struggle and rewarded him with a kiss full on the lips.

"Go get your coat," Aaron said, holding up the envelope. "We're going to see *Gone With the Wind!*"

Now it was Aaron's turn to be kissed, this time from a joyous Lisa.

"I've wanted to see that for ages!" she cried, and, waiting while Gina ran to tell her employer, she and Aaron clasped hands and giggled at Gunter, who remained crimson.

"Look at him blush!" Lisa teased.

Gina ran out the door, scarf trailing behind her. "Let's go!" she cried. "I don't want to miss one minute!"

They took the underground to Portobello Road, to pass the time before the show began. They rambled through the bustling streets of the outdoor flea market, where vendors were selling old clothes, jewelry, pots and pans, books, tools, and the like. A noisy Punch-and-Judy show was performed out of the back of a cart, and for a penny a throw, you could "Knock Hitler's Block Off."

Gina chattered on about the noisy kids she was taking care of, and Lisa, in turn, relayed all the Willesden gossip—about her audition, the battle over the Victrola, and the hole in the ceiling of the girls' bathroom.

Lisa was surprised to see how well Aaron knew his way around the flea market, guiding his friends down the narrow, crowded streets. He stopped several times to talk with shop owners, and more than once she heard "Mr. Lewin! Mr. Lewin!" called out.

"You're very popular," she said finally.

"Just a little business deal," he answered, happy to be mysterious.

Realizing it was getting late, they raced to Piccadilly Circus and joined the weekend crowds stepping over rubble and bomb craters on their way to the theaters and cinemas. They spotted the enormous marquee with the names Vivien Leigh and Clark Gable and the full-color posters of Scarlett O'Hara swooning in Rhett's arms, and they ran as fast as they could, making it to their seats just as the lights were dimming.

A spotlight came up on the organist who launched into "White Cliffs of Dover." The audience joined in, clapping and singing.

When the four of them began to squirm with anticipation, the theater lights finally went down and the newsreel came on. Everyone cheered as tough battalions of British soldiers were shown marching through North Africa to fight Rommel's forces in the desert. The Brits looked unbeatable.

Then came pictures of the home front—London digging out from the bombings, emergency crews pulling a patient from the ruins, housewives lining up to recycle pots and pans. King George and Queen Elizabeth inspected the ruins of Parliament and looked for all the world as though they were dressed for a garden party. Churchill walked through devastated streets in his homburg, determined and tough.

The newsreel continued with films of a busy factory scene. Gunter suddenly stood up. "That's where I work!" he blurted out.

"Shhh!" Gina said, putting her hand over his mouth.

But Gunter couldn't be contained. He turned around to the strangers behind him. "I work there!" he exclaimed.

"Down in front!" someone yelled, throwing an empty candy box at him. Gunter took the hint and slid back down into his seat.

Finally, it was time for the main feature.

Lisa was mesmerized by Scarlett O'Hara and her troubles. Her heart raced as she watched the heroine struggle with hunger and war and desperation. She sobbed into her handkerchief as Scarlett swore that "as God is my witness" she would never let her family go hungry again. At times it was hard to focus on the movie, her mind kept racing back to her family in Vienna, remembering how difficult it had been to get food, imagining how difficult it must be now.

When the film was over, Lisa was weeping so hard that she could hardly get up. But once again she rallied her considerable will. I'm going to make it, she said to herself, echoing the heroine's words. Just like Scarlett . . . by hook or by crook . . . I'm going to make it through.

18

$\mathcal{L}$ISA'S PERSISTENT practicing was an inspiration for the others. In the fall, Edith enrolled in a shorthand course, determined as well "to make something of herself." Gunter begged his boss, Mr. Steinberg, to make good on his statement that he was "crucial to the war effort" and received a promotion to the accounting department. Not to be left out, Hans enrolled in a course to become a physical therapist and brought home pounds and pounds of braille anatomy books to study. And Johnny wrote more and more poetry, declaring that Lisa's music had convinced him to become a writer after the war.

Only Aaron, it seemed to Lisa, didn't join in the "hard work brigade." He showed up late several times a week and had to throw pebbles at the third-floor window so Gunter would come down and let him in. If he was lucky, Mrs. Cohen wouldn't hear; occasionally she did.

"Mr. Lewin! I've told you a dozen times I won't tolerate another curfew violation," the matron said harshly, coming out of her room in her dressing gown late one night. "Not only is it dangerous for you, but it's extremely rude to those of us who need our sleep. This is not a hotel, Mr. Lewin, this is a refugee hostel, and I expect your coopera- tion or I expect you to find another place to live. Do I make myself understood?" The matron had never made good on her threats, but her patience was wearing thin.

"Yes, Mrs. Cohen, it won't happen again," Aaron prom- ised, his mischievous smile replaced by a convenient earnestness. He had made this promise many times before.

"What is that you're carrying?" she asked.

Aaron had been careful to hide most of the things he had brought home, but this time he was caught in the act. He handed her the package—it was a box of chocolates.

"Mr. Lewin, I would be very disappointed if I thought you were in any way participating in the black market. It would be most ungrateful and unpatriotic; rationing is how we will win the war!"

"I got them as a bonus for staying overtime," he said smoothly. "I brought them to share with everybody."

Mrs. Cohen didn't believe him for a second. "Then I ex- pect you to put them in the kitchen, Mr. Lewin. Good night!" She turned on her heels and slammed her door.

Aaron hid his angry expression from the matron. He was tired of explaining himself all the time; most of all, he was tired of being treated like a child. He heard the muf- fled sounds of Lisa practicing in the basement and headed down the hall.

She lifted her head and smiled when she heard the door open and saw him on the stairs.

"That's enough practicing, come on up for a while," Aaron said.

"I'm not finished yet, I can't," she said, shouting above her playing.

"Come on, Lisa! Is music all you can think about?"

"Right now, yes! I don't have much time until the audition. I have to practice."

"You've got months!"

"Aaron! It's important to me."

"And I'm not important?" he demanded, frustrated.

"Of course you're important, but not right now!"

"Fine, suit yourself," Aaron answered angrily, and slammed the cellar door.

"Aaron!" she yelled after him, but he had already gone. She returned to the piece she was practicing and pounded the keys with even more fury. When she was totally exhausted, she went up into the living room and found Aaron sulking on the couch. She went and sat next to him, putting her arm around him for the inevitable reconciliation.

Through it all was the constant threat of the bombings. Some weeks were worse than others. The headlines would scream, 1,000 DEAD IN ONE HELLISH NIGHT! Then the next day, the retaliation, RAF FLYBOYS BATTER THE RUHR. Back and forth the destruction went.

When the whine of the air raid sirens began, Lisa no longer had to scurry next door to the convent; she could stay behind in her protected basement and hammer the octaves of the ending of the ballade. The louder the screams of the bombers, the louder she played. Neighbors on Willesden Lane would hear the eerie sound of classical music emanating from the basement and do double takes as they hurried to their shelters.

In the midst of the chaos, Lisa kept to her disciplined

schedule, practicing and practicing. Progress wasn't always guaranteed, however; she was having terrible trouble with the coda of the ballade. She stared at the mass of black notes in front of her and tried to will her fingers to find the right path through the keys. All she had to rely upon were the images her mother had taught her, so she conjured up a scene from the life of Chopin, which her mother had described. She visualized a romantic young Chopin leaving his native Poland behind forever and wept as she saw him in his carriage, fleeing the flames that consumed his beloved Warsaw. She played a somber passage with feeling, but often her fingers couldn't figure out the intricacies, and she would call out, "Mama! I need your help," then begin the passage over again.

One evening, Hans noticed that she was going over and over the opening of the piece, then stopping and beginning again. Why do you always stop there?" he asked.

"My mother always said that the opening and closing of a piece were the most important. They'll forget the middle," she said confidently.

"That's ridiculous, they won't forget the middle if you play it poorly!" Hans shot back. "Come on, play me the whole piece all the way through."

She looked at him as if he were crazy. "I don't know all of it yet," she answered.

"I'll let you use the music."

Lisa snarled at him silently, then played through the entire piece. When she looked up at the end, Hans was frowning.

"Now what's wrong?" she asked, upset, assuming he was going to be impressed by her progress.

"Too many liberties, too much rubato. Keep the rhythm steady," Hans counseled.

This was the worst criticism Lisa could hear because it was the exact same complaint Professor Isseles had had time and time again.

"I'm not a machine!" she shot back defensively. "The music is passionate. It's important to let my emotions come through!"

"But you must have a consistent beat. No matter how beautifully you play a melody, you have to have something to hang it on."

"Since when did you become a music teacher?" she asked, throwing the music on the floor and stamping up the staircase. She ran into Gunter, who was on his way down.

"Don't tell me the concert is over already," he said, disappointed.

"Leave me alone!" Lisa said, slamming the door behind her on the way out.

Two days later, Gunter and Hans handed Lisa a box wrapped in newspaper. "It's from Hans, and me, and the rest of the hostel," Gunter said.

"What is it?"

"Open it and find out."

Inside the box was a metronome. She pulled out the pyramid-shaped device and set it on the piano. Gunter, laughing, started it ticking.

"What is this, a conspiracy?" she said, joining them laughing. "I'm sorry, fellows, I promise not to have any more tantrums. You're right, Hans, I need it. Thank you."

The next crisis came when Hans asked Aaron to reread the mimeographed sheets from the Royal Academy and double-check the repertoire requirements. Horrified by what Aaron read, he confronted Lisa that night at dinner.

"Lisa, you didn't read all the requirements!" Hans said.

"Of course I did. What are you talking about?"

"You will be tested on sight-reading, solfeggio, and fundamentals of music theory," Hans said. "Aaron read me the rest of the application."

"I, ah, didn't think it really mattered," she stammered, concentrating on the plateful of noodles before her.

"Of course it matters!"

"I'm terrible at all those things, and I'll never learn them anyway. I know my only chance is to enchant the judges with my playing," Lisa said, trying to sound as confident as she could.

Gunter, Aaron, and Hans were silent. They weren't buying it, which infuriated Lisa further.

"Well?" she continued. "I know what I can do, and I know what I can't do . . . Besides, solfeggio won't help my Chopin!"

The boys shook their heads. Lisa kept eating, trying to paste a defiant look on her face.

Hans said finally, "It doesn't work that way in England. If you fail the fundamentals, they won't give you the scholarship. That's all there is to it."

"I can't learn all of that so quickly!" Lisa begged.

"Yes, you can," Gunter said. "You've got until February!"

"We're going to help you," added Aaron.

"And that's all there is to it," Hans said with finality.

The next two months were dedicated to sight-reading and fundamentals. Every night, after a long day at the factory, Lisa would hurry through her afternoon practice and, after a quick dinner, go back to the basement for the dreaded hour of instruction.

Hans was in charge of sight-reading. Since he had memorized every note of his own sheet music, he would instruct Aaron to choose a piece that Lisa hadn't seen before but which he knew perfectly. Then Hans would set the metronome to a slow and steady beat.

"All right, look at the key signature and think ahead one measure. Ready? Go!" Hans clapped his hands once and off she went. Some nights the sheet music ended up on the floor, other nights on top of the pickle jars.

"Pretty funny, huh? A blind guy teaching you sight-reading!" Hans yelled over the music. "Ouch, that would be F-sharp there, Lisa."

"At least you're not deaf!" Lisa shot back, and they laughed until their stomachs hurt.

Music theory was Aaron's bailiwick. He finally admitted to Lisa that he had studied the violin in Mannheim and had learned the basics of dominants, subdominants, and chord inversions. Science came easily to him, and he patiently digested and explained (from a newly acquired textbook) the principles of harmony.

"I wish I had known that before," she marveled. "Oh! I get it!" she would say. They would lie together on the couch in the living room, Glenn Miller blaring from the radio, and she would guess her way through the chord changes—"Dominant, tonic, seventh"—as the swing music filled the air.

Solfeggio was a trial for everybody. Lisa's singing voice wasn't particularly inspiring, and do, re, mi, fa, sol, la, ti, do wasn't a very pleasing tune. On behalf of the entire hostel, Edith finally insisted that do, re, mi, be a "basement only" activity.

*   *   *

The weather turned cold and damp; winter had come. The Wehrmacht had continued rolling over Europe, taking Kiev and moving toward Moscow.

Coal was severely rationed, and soon the hostel had none left. But Lisa continued playing in the freezing basement no matter what. The audition was in two months and she still had so much to learn. She would come home from work, bundle up warmly, and go to the kitchen to stretch her anxious fingers over the wood-burning stove. She then descended into the cellar, which was so damp that the moisture condensed on the walls and some nights she could see her breath as she exhaled. Sometimes her fingers ached terribly; other times Mrs. Cohen would hear her coughing and beg her to come up to the warmth of the kitchen. Lisa seldom agreed, coming up only every once in a while out of respect for the matron. And when she did, she stayed only for a moment, then rushed back down to her piano.

In spite of the frost of one of the coldest winters on record, Londoners ventured tentatively into parks and onto sidewalks, betting that the bombs would continue to fall only at night.

Sundays, Aaron would convince her to stroll down Oxford Street and look in the windows, as in the old days. Harvey Nichols had strange-looking fashions, and one display had a full rubberized body suit with matching gas mask. Blitz clothing became the new fashion.

One day, unexpectedly, Gina arrived at the hostel. "I'm back!" was all she said in explanation, and took off chatting as much as always. She had managed to get a job as a beautician and was able to give up her posh nanny job in Richmond. Although she found such common work demeaning, it was worth it to return to her friends at 243

Willesden Lane. They were all glad to see her, especially Gunter, who walked around with a moony grin for days. Gina confided to Lisa that Gunter's smile made combing strangers' hair worth the step down in status. In no time, the two girlfriends were back sharing late-night confidences about life and love. Most nights, Gina lay face up on the bed, smiling from ear to ear, while Lisa coiled on her side lamenting Aaron's ornery streak. His attitude problem had gotten worse.

One evening, the argument between Mrs. Cohen and Aaron was particularly heated. Whether it was the new edict she had received from Bloomsbury about stricter rules for curfew or Aaron's insolent attitude, her patience had finally run out.

"If you come back after curfew, you're not to come back at all."

"Fine, have it your way," Aaron said, and went into the basement to let off steam. He tried to get Lisa's sympathy—to no avail.

"Mrs. Cohen is right, you idiot! You've got to be more serious. You're always fooling around," Lisa lectured.

"You're sounding awfully high and mighty!" Aaron said, and turned and walked out.

Lisa went back to practicing but after a few minutes found herself filled with regret and ran upstairs to the living room to find Aaron and apologize.

He was nowhere to be found, so she returned to the basement and her Bach.

The next night, Lisa was devastated when Aaron still had not returned. Lisa lay on her bed, contrite and worried. "It's all my fault," she moaned.

Gina looked on. "Don't worry, he used to do this lots of times before you came. He'll be back."

But Aaron didn't come back the next night, nor the night after. Lisa lay on her bed at the call for lights-out, her body racked by coughing.

"Maybe you should stop practicing for a while, Lisa. It's too cold down there," Gina suggested, concerned.

"It's just a cough, it will go away, don't worry."

"If it doesn't go away soon, we won't get any sleep," Gina said, only half joking.

On the third night, the telephone in the hallway rang, and the girls heard Mrs. Cohen's footsteps on the stairs.

"Lisa?" the matron called. "It's Aaron Lewin—on the telephone."

Lisa jumped up and ran downstairs, grabbing the receiver. "Aaron, Aaron, are you all right?"

Gina crept down the stairs and listened to her friend as she clutched the telephone to her ear.

"What? For how long?" Lisa cried out, alarmed. "Wait, wait, don't hang up! Aaron? Aaron?" she shouted. The receiver went dead in her hand.

"He only had a one-minute call," she said in disbelief to the matron and Gina as they approached.

"What happened?" they asked in unison.

"Aaron's been arrested! And sent to the Isle of Man—as an alien!"

"Oh, my God, for how long?" Gina asked.

"I d-don't know," Lisa stammered.

Mrs. Cohen took the receiver and hung it back on the hook. "It was bound to happen to him sooner or later. You have to admit he was asking for it."

As tears sprang to Lisa's eyes, Mrs. Cohen put her arm around the distraught teenager. "It won't be forever. Now, go upstairs, dear, try to get some sleep."

Lisa disentangled herself from Mrs. Cohen's awkward

embrace, ran up the staircase, and threw herself on the covers of her ice-cold bed. Her sobs turned into a fit of coughing.

Gina stood over her friend, worried. "Why don't I see if Mrs. Cohen could make you some hot water and lemon or something?"

"He doesn't deserve it! Why would he deserve it? She must hate him."

"She didn't mean anything. Of course he doesn't deserve it."

"It's all my fault!"

"Why is it your fault? Lots of the boys are getting picked up. Look at Paul!" Gina said with as much sympathy as she could muster at that time of night.

Lisa kept mumbling to herself, not listening. "It's all my fault. If only I hadn't been so mean he wouldn't have left. Aaron's right, the only thing I think about is my music."

"It's not your fault, and besides, Paul said it wasn't so bad in the camp, remember?" Gina added.

"What do you know about it!" Lisa exploded, jumping out of bed and slamming the door behind her. Gina could hear the sounds of Lisa throwing things behind the bathroom door.

How was she going to live without Aaron?

December was miserable for Lisa. She practiced as hard as ever, but the relentless cold had no warm embrace at the end of the evening. Aaron sent several postcards, apologizing for being so careless, but his brief words made her miss him even more.

Lisa's cough got worse; it was so bad that sometimes Mrs. Cohen could hear it through the closed door of the cellar. One night, as Mrs. Cohen stood at the top of the stairs and listened to the alarming sound, she got an idea. She went to the telephone and made a call.

The following evening, as Lisa was playing a lyrical passage from the *Pathétique*, she heard a knock at the door. It opened slightly and a familiar face poked through the opening.

"Lisa? May I come in?" said Mrs. Canfield.

"Oh, hello!" Lisa said, surprised. "Yes, please, come on down."

Mrs. Canfield stepped carefully down the steps, followed by Johnny, who was carrying a small, old-fashioned coal-burning stove. Lisa recognized it from her house on Riffel Road.

"I can't accept this," Lisa protested.

"Nonsense," said the Quaker lady. "You'll catch your death down here."

"What will you use at home?"

"I have plenty of jumpers and coats. I don't need it."

"I really appreciate it, but I just can't," Lisa insisted.

"You can and you will," Mrs. Canfield said in an unyielding tone.

Lisa finally relented. "Thank you," she said gratefully. She hadn't wanted to admit how weak she had been feeling of late, and the warmth certainly would help.

Johnny lit the stove, and when he was sure it was functioning properly, stood up and handed her a folded sheet of paper. She opened it quickly, saw it was a poem, and smiled. "Thank you, Johnny, I'll keep it on the piano to inspire me!"

"Be well, be warm!" Johnny called out on his way back up the stairs.

"Would thee mind if I stayed and listened?" Mrs. Canfield asked.

"Oh yes, please do," Lisa replied.

Mrs. Canfield pulled out the knitting bag she had brought, leaned back in her chair, and smiled. Soon the basement was almost toasty, and the walls and bottles became coated with condensation as the dampness was replaced by a pleasing warmth. Lisa insisted on leaving the door open to the kitchen so some of it could escape to help the others.

She began the Beethoven *Pathétique*, her fingers moving with a new freedom over the warm keys.

"Ah, thank you, Lisa—what a comfort your beautiful music is."

An hour later, earlier than usual, the air raid siren went off. Both Lisa and Mrs. Canfield were surprised; it had been several weeks since there had been a bombing. Mrs. Canfield got up to head for her shelter around the corner.

"Oh, no, you must stay, ma'am. It's too cold for you in your backyard." Lisa shivered, remembering the dreadful nights in the corrugated prison in Mrs. Canfield's garden.

"Thank you, child, I think I will," Mrs. Canfield said, going up the stairs to secure the door. She picked up her knitting again and listened to Lisa scare away the bombers with her chords.

Usually the "all clear" siren would sound several hours later, but this night was an exception. Hour after hour, the scream of the bombers came over them: no amount of pounding from the basement could chase the noise away. Lisa began to cough and couldn't stop, so she huddled by the stove under a blanket next to Mrs. Canfield, who put her arm around her. Suddenly tired of being brave all the time, Lisa began to cry.

"What is wrong, my dear?" Mrs. Canfield asked.

"Sometimes I miss my family so much that I feel I can't

go on . . . I can't go on without them. I don't even know why I should go on without them."

Mrs. Canfield hugged the trembling girl tight. "It is not for thee to decide," she said. "Ultimately, God is in charge of our world. We have been placed here to do his will. I believe it is his will for thee to play your music. I hear a great truth in it."

"My mother told me to always hold on to my music."

"You must go forward with that in your heart, Lisa. Listen to your beloved mother."

Finally, the all clear blared, and Mrs. Canfield looked at her watch. It was five in the morning. She helped Lisa up the stairs, and they walked out of the hostel into the bitter cold dawn. Willesden Lane had been spared, but it seemed as though the rest of London were burning. Were the Nazis coming? Lisa wondered in a sudden delirium. She felt herself go limp.

The next thing she remembered was waking up in her bunk bed as Gina handed her a hot cup of chicken soup.

"You're awake! You're awake . . . oh, Lisa, we were so worried!" Gina cried, and ran out to spread the word.

Mrs. Cohen arrived upstairs in an instant. "You gave us quite a fright, dear," she said with a slightly scolding tone. "The doctor has confined you to bed rest for the next week; he says you have a bad bronchitis."

"A what?" Lisa cried with alarm, not understanding the word.

"Bronchitis, a very bad cough. You're not to get up."

"But I have to practice," Lisa said.

"Not until you're better, that's an order."

Gina was anxious to get her turn. She wanted to tell Lisa everything that was going on. "You've been asleep for

197

two whole days. You've missed everything!" she blurted out.

"Gina!" Mrs. Cohen interrupted. "Let Lisa rest, please."

"No, Mrs. Cohen, I want to know what's going on. Have the Nazis come?" she asked fearfully.

"The Nazis? No, silly! The Yanks are coming! You slept through the bombing of Pearl Harbor!"

"Pearl what?" Lisa asked, totally confused.

"The Americans have joined the war," the matron explained. "We'll tell you all about it later, dear."

Suddenly, Gina hung her head and started to cry.

"What's wrong, please tell me!" Lisa asked.

"Hush, Gina, we must let Lisa rest," said Mrs. Cohen.

"It's Johnny," Gina said, paying no attention to the matron.

"Johnny? What has happened?"

"Gina!" Mrs. Cohen repeated sternly.

"Please tell me. Is he dead?" Lisa whispered.

"He's been badly hurt. A wall gave way in a building where he was helping to put out a fire. He is fighting bravely in the hospital and wants to be remembered to all of us, and to you especially, Lisa," Mrs. Cohen explained.

"He may lose his legs, though," Gina added sadly.

Tears streamed from Lisa's eyes. "Oh, no! Can I go see him?" she asked.

"You are not to get out of bed," the matron said firmly.

Lisa turned away from them to control her emotions. What a terrible thing this war is, she thought as she prayed for her friend.

19

$\mathcal{T}$WO WEEKS of bed rest cured Lisa's fever, but her cough lingered. The audition date was fast approaching, so despite Mrs. Cohen's reservations, she resumed a modified practice schedule.

Her support staff redoubled its efforts: Gunter took over Aaron's duties and quizzed her on theory, Gina suffered through the do-re-mi's, and Hans listened to her interpretation. Three weeks and counting; so far, so good. Hans even ventured that Aaron's absence lent her music a depth well beyond her seventeen years. "Ah, now that's Chopin!"

The week before the audition, Lisa skipped her Monday evening practice and went to see Johnny in the hospital. She picked a giant stalk of hollyhocks from the convent garden and set out on the journey alone. The ward was filled with civilian casualties as well as injured police and fire personnel. Some had plaster casts, others were burn victims, their limbs totally wrapped in gauze. Johnny, pale and visibly thinner, had been confined to his bed and the head nurse told Lisa that her visit would have to be kept short.

He smiled when she approached, and she kissed him on the forehead. "Oh, Johnny, I've missed you!"

"You've stolen all the nun's flowers. Shame on you!" His banter covered his emotion, but his expression didn't lie about how happy he was to see her.

They chatted about life at the hostel, and she went on about the hours of practicing and the excruciating lessons with the committee in the cellar. She saw how Johnny loved hearing the news. He wanted to know every detail. She asked about his poetry but didn't have the heart to question him about his legs.

"So are you ready?" he asked.

"For what?" she joked, as if she didn't know that everyone, not just herself, was counting down the hours to the audition.

"What will you play first?"

"The Chopin."

"Good choice, although it's so powerful it will be hard to follow."

"Hmm, maybe you're right," she said, smiling.

They were interrupted by the ward nurse, who let them know that visiting hours were over.

"Before we say good-bye, I have a request," Johnny said gravely. "When you play the Chopin, will you think of me?"

"Only if you give me another poem," she teased.

Johnny put his head back slowly, closed his eyes, and began reciting softly.

> *Tell me, what does God hear?*
> *I have despaired of prayers with words*
> *All of my prayers are your music.*

Lisa took his huge hands in her own, smiling at the contrast in size. "Of course I'll think of you, Johnny. I only wish I could play it for you right now."

"You don't have to, all I have to do is close my eyes and I can hear it." Lisa kissed him gently and left.

With three days to go before the audition, Lisa was little good to Mrs. McRae or Mr. Dimble at the factory; she would fret about her playing and chatter nervously about her insecurities.

"I'll be up against students from the finest families in England," she complained. "And I don't even have a decent dress to wear."

"That's a shame, isn't it," Mrs. McRae commented dryly.

Lisa realized with remorse how frivolous she must sound to this woman who had lost her husband in the war, and tried to get to work with no further complaints.

So it was with surprise that Lisa came to work the next morning and found a package, tied with recycled string, sitting on her chair.

"What's this?" she asked.

Several of the other ladies stood up and gathered around, saying nothing.

Mrs. McRae looked up from her work with a mischievous grin, as if she didn't understand the question.

So Lisa picked it up and unwrapped it carefully. She pulled out a beautiful dark blue dress. "Mrs. McRae, you didn't . . ." Stunned, Lisa held up the elegant new dress and the ladies around her clapped.

"Very fancy, that is, Mrs. McRae!" a co-worker said. "Next thing you know, you'll be seamstress to the queen!"

Mrs. McRae smiled proudly. "That'll impress 'em, I hope."

"Oh, thank you! Thank you!" Lisa threw her arms around the woman.

The Saturday before the audition, Lisa worked alone in the cellar, having told Hans that she needed time for quiet reflection. She practiced slowly, softly, with intense concentration, every note taking on a depth and significance. She went over and over the coda of the ballade, sometimes elated by her mastery of it, at other times terrified that she was out of control.

Then, in one of the soft passages, she heard a familiar whistling coming from the kitchen. It was the Grieg! She leapt up.

Could it be? Had Aaron miraculously come back to wish her luck? She ran to the top of the stairs only to find Gunter! She tried to hide her disappointment as he laughed at her confusion and handed her a letter from Aaron.

She tore open the letter and raced quickly through his words. Aaron was uncharacteristically positive, almost chatty, and convinced that he would be released soon.

He urged her on: "Don't waste a single second thinking of me. Know that I love you and concentrate on the audition. I'll be thinking of you every moment."

She reread the last line a second time, filled with joy, and then threw herself with added fervor back into the Beethoven.

The night before the audition, Lisa had a dream. She was riding on the streetcar through the streets of Vienna in the days before the Nazis. The car passed the Ferris wheel in the Prater, and Lisa saw its merry lights going around and around. She saw the stately statues, and monumental buildings, and waved at the little band playing in the park. She glided past St. Stephen's Cathedral and found herself on Professor Isseles's street. He was waving at her from the window and smiling proudly. She heard his reassuring voice in her ear: "What have you prepared for me today, Miss Jura? Shall we begin?"

When she awoke, she did not feel nervous or frightened. She was clearheaded and felt a great calm within her. She trusted that the music itself would be her strength, her best friend, as her mother had said it would be. She reached into her dresser and pulled out the pictures of her parents, now tied together with a satin ribbon. "Wish me luck, Mama . . . Papa." She kissed the picture and began her preparations.

The long line outside the girls' bathroom grew loud and cranky—inside, Gina struggled to achieve just the right hairstyle for her friend's big day. She was determined to style Lisa's hair in a sophisticated swirl of curls that landed just left of the top of her head, where she pinned it securely into place with bobby pins.

The line of girls clapped when the two girls finally left the bathroom, as much in relief at finally being allowed their turn as for the beautiful vision of elegance that Lisa had become. She twirled in Mrs. McRae's dress, took an exaggerated bow, and ran downstairs.

Mrs. Cohen and the cook appeared in the foyer, wiping their hands on their aprons, and waved good-bye. When Mrs. Glazer saw the beautiful girl in her fancy new dress, she burst into tears.

"I feel like it's my own daughter," she whispered as she waved.

Mrs. Cohen took out her handkerchief and handed it to the cook.

Lisa was surprised to see Gunter waiting on the sidewalk. He was wearing the brown tweed suit, which was now a size too small for him. "Aren't you late for work?" she asked.

"I'm going with you," he responded cheerfully.

"Gunter!" she protested.

"The hat factory has given me the day off."

"Gunter, you don't have to, I'll be fine."

"Of course I do," he said. "I'm going to quiz you on the way."

She laughed and took his arm. "All right, then, thank you." She knew this was a conspiracy that had been concocted by the committee.

"The dress looks very beautiful on you," Gunter added as they hurried off to the underground.

"If this dress could play the Beethoven sonata," she joked, "I'd have nothing to worry about."

As they rode the train, Gunter thumbed through the pages of the textbook, lobbing question after question.

"Describe the sonata form. . . . What is counterpoint? . . . Give me an example of polyphony. . . ."

She did her best to answer each one, and when she stumbled on polyphony, she dismissed the question with a wave of her hand, insisting: "That's not important!"

Gunter gave her a scolding look, then continued with the drill until they reached their stop.

Lisa hadn't really felt nervous until they arrived at the entrance to the Royal Academy of Music. She was once again overwhelmed by the grandeur of the building. She saw the large group of well-dressed English teenagers and their parents and felt the bottom drop out of her stomach. She could feel the atmosphere of intense competition enveloping the courtyard. She had known she would be up against a number of young and talented musicians, but she hadn't imagined how many.

They joined the line and Gunter tugged on his wool trousers in a reflex gesture, trying to fill the two-inch gap between his cuff and his shoes. Lisa smoothed the material of her blue dress neatly over her hips.

The boys next to them looked cool and confident, well scrubbed and manicured, and some of them sported public school ties and expensive shoes. Their parents hovered close to them, projecting an aura of English nonchalance and superiority.

The girls were even more intimidating; most wore simple but elegant black dresses, often accented by a single strand of pearls. They emitted a collective glow of beauty and confidence. Although she had tried to imagine the worst, Lisa had not prepared herself for the polished appearance of these teenagers, who were so unlike her refugee compatriots at the hostel or her co-workers at the factory.

But what made her feel most apart from the others wasn't the fact that she had a blue dress and not a black one. It was that she was the only aspiring artist in line on this important day who wasn't accompanied by his parents.

Don't worry, Mama, she said silently. I know you're here.

Gunter saw that Lisa was shaking and took her hand

and held it tightly. She smiled at her loyal friend, so glad that he was here.

After what seemed like an eternity, a young woman with a clipboard came forward.

"Piano students will be next; follow me, please," she said, reading off a list of names. Lisa's was among them, and the young woman signaled for them to follow her. Gunter released her hand, giving her the RAF thumbs-up they had seen in the newsreels, and disappeared into the foyer to wait with the rest of the families.

Lisa and twenty other students were taken to a small classroom on the third floor, where she was handed a pencil and a test booklet and told she had one hour to complete the music theory portion of the exam. The pages were filled with endless questions. Nervous that she was spending too much time on each, she began to speed through them in a flurry. Answers that she had crammed so hastily into her head appeared before her like visions, and she wrote them down at a furious pace, afraid they might disappear like the popping of a soap bubble. There were questions she couldn't answer, but then there were many she could, and she alternated between the feeling that she was doing brilliantly and the fear that she was failing miserably. She answered the questions so fast that she finished the exam early but felt too scared to go back and check things, afraid she would get confused.

"Pencils down," the monitor said finally, then she was taken to a practice room with an upright piano, where she was tested on pitch and solfeggio by a serious young man. She sang the intervals as asked and did her best to name the notes as he struck them on the keyboard.

"Thank you," he said when it was over, not giving any

hint of how she had done. "Please wait in the hallway out-side the auditorium on the first floor."

.The merciful young woman with the clipboard came by and told her that she would be sixth in line for the per-formance section of the audition. She was relieved to know the order. At least she wouldn't have her heart in her throat each time the auditorium doors swung open and a new student was called.

When Gunter saw her he came over and sat in the chair beside her. She smiled at him and leaned her head back against the wall and did her mental preparation. She or-ganized the images of each piece in her head and tried to center herself for the trial ahead of her.

She knew that the audition would be only twenty min-utes and that the judges might interrupt her, in order to hear bits of all that she had been asked to prepare.

Occasionally the furious pounding of a competitor's strong octaves could be heard through the padded doors, ruining her concentration. Each pianist sounded more magnificent than the one before. She tried to force the sounds from her head; the more she heard, the less confi-dent she felt.

When the woman with the clipboard called out her name, Lisa stood up as proudly as she could, disguising the sudden pounding of her heart, and walked through the double doors.

Her knees were weak as she walked down the corridor of the cavernous auditorium toward the stage, where a beautiful Steinway grand piano lay waiting. In the tenth row of the otherwise empty hall, three judges sat waiting with impassive expressions.

She climbed the stairs, walked over to the piano, and bowed to the judges. She had planned to begin with the ballade in order to dazzle them from the beginning, but with the pounding of her heart terrorizing her so, she decided to switch to the Beethoven. Maybe the steady march of the opening chords would calm her down.

"What would you like to play first?" the male judge on the left called out, his voice echoing through the empty hall.

"Beethoven's Piano Sonata in C Minor, opus thirteen, number eight," Lisa replied.

"The *Pathétique*," the other man said, jotting down a note in the book in front of him.

She adjusted her weight on the piano bench, tested the pedals quickly to judge their spring, took a deep breath, and began.

The opening notes of the sonata were solemn, the tempo measured and deliberate. For Lisa, it was a call to prayer. It was as profound and heartfelt as the lighting of the candles on her parents' mantelpiece. She saw the care in her mother's hands as she kindled the flame of Shabbat, and relived the warmth of the glowing dining room in the harmonies of the dramatic chords.

Then out of the gravity of this call to prayer came the energy and bustle of the con brio. Her hands flew lightly into the trills and arpeggios, speeding up and down the keyboard. She imagined the energy was like the preparations for the Sabbath meal. She saw the playfulness of her sister Sonia scurrying in and out with the plates—how fast she went on her excited little legs as the high notes tinkled and twirled through the acoustical perfection of the hall.

Again the solemnity of Beethoven's music returned with the reprise of its opening chords. In the majestic simplicity of the notes, Lisa's hands searched for just the right touch to convey the poignant melancholy that lay within her.

"Thank you," she heard between the notes near the end of the first movement. She suddenly realized that the judges had let her go on for ten whole minutes. Oh, no, she thought, that means only ten minutes to go and I haven't shown them the ballade!

"Perhaps you could play your prelude and fugue next."

She wanted to say: "No, no, you must hear the Chopin!" But she bowed graciously and began Bach's Fugue in D Minor. She tried hard to hear the metronome in her head, since she knew the piece should be precise and controlled. She tried to be careful, but as the beautiful tones of the Steinway rang gracefully from her delicate touch, she couldn't help but add a liberty here, a little rubato there. She thought she was doing pretty well when the woman's thin voice pierced her concentration.

"Thank you," said the small lady in the dark suit. "And what have you prepared from the Romantic period?"

"I will play Chopin's Ballade in G Minor, opus twenty-three, number one."

Again no reaction, just the movement of pens making notes in their mysterious books.

As with the Beethoven, the Chopin opened slowly and majestically—a largo. But then Chopin opened Lisa's heart with his romantic, interlaced melodies. Here was a composer who reached into the furthest recesses of Lisa's soul and stirred her deepest yearnings.

Lisa's mother had told her that in this ballade, Chopin was crying for the loss of his native Poland—at having to flee war and destruction, never to return. It was a tribute to his lost homeland. Lisa's fingers sang her own nostalgic tribute—to Vienna, now lost to her, and to her parents and Rosie, and even Sonia, so far from her.

She laid her heart bare as her fingers moved almost with no conscious effort. At one point, she realized that a tear was falling down her cheek, but she paid it no mind.

As she played deeper into the ballade, Chopin's music wove lighthearted arpeggios from the haunting melody. Lisa's strong but delicate fingers raced up and down the keyboard and flew through filigreed chromatics as she expressed the passionate yearnings for her future life—her growing feelings for Aaron, her prayer for Johnny's recovery, and her belief in the beauty of a world someday without war.

She was in such a state of ecstatic unconsciousness that at the end of the fiery conclusion of the pounding octaves of the *presto con fuoco*, she hardly knew where she was.

Another "Thank you" broke into her reverie, and she realized with alarm that she had played the entire piece without being interrupted. Maybe they had tried to stop her and she hadn't heard them. How embarrassing!

She raised her head and looked out. The male judges were writing in their books, and the tiny woman nodded her head politely.

They don't look angry, I guess, Lisa thought, but these were the only words of encouragement she could find to give herself. She scoured their faces for a reaction but found none.

"That is all, you may go," was all she got by way of response, so she bowed politely and walked off the stage with as much dignity as she could muster.

Gunter was waiting in the hallway. "How was it? How did you do?" he asked, anxious for the news.

"I did everything I could. I gave it my all."

20

FEBRUARY BECAME March, but the weather in the spring of 1942 remained bitterly cold. The bombings grew more sporadic as the unusually icy weather made it more difficult for the Luftwaffe to fly as far as London. Lisa started working overtime at the factory—as much to do her patriotic duty as to distract herself from the agony of waiting for the results of the audition.

She trudged down the block every morning, passing the same newsboy on the corner of Walm Lane, and read the daily ration of gloomy news, It was true the Americans had given everyone a huge boost in morale, but the news from Europe continued to be grim—frightening rumors were circulating at the synagogue about the massive deportations of all Jews from Europe.

Mail call at dinner was a sad time since most of the children had stopped receiving letters from their parents in Europe. They had now transferred their expectations to waiting for Lisa's answer from the Royal Academy of Music.

Each night at dinner, there was a hush if Lisa's name was called.

"Lisa Jura?" Mrs. Cohen would say, looking at the handwriting on the envelope.

Breaths would be held.

"It's from your sister, Sonia . . . again," Mrs. Cohen would add quickly, to relieve the unbearable tension.

Sonia's letters were now written in fluent English and filled with more positive news about what she had learned in school.

One Friday night, at the Shabbat meal, Lisa thought she detected a strange excitement. More than a few heads turned to look her way. She knew that often, whoever had taken in the mail spread the gossip of who had a letter waiting, and such news traveled like wildfire.

But no one had said anything to her, so why were they all looking at her so strangely? she wondered.

"Lisa Jura?" Mrs. Cohen said, holding up a letter. "It's from the London Royal Academy of Music." A hush came over the room.

As was the custom, Mrs. Cohen handed the envelope to the boy on her left, who passed it around the large dining room table. Each person gently stroked the embossed gold letters of the Royal Academy emblem with their eager fingers. When the letter made its way to Lisa, she took it and stared, paralyzed.

"Aren't you going to open it?" Mrs. Cohen questioned gently.

Lisa could not respond, she kept staring at the envelope before her. Could she face another disappointment?

"Would you like me to open it?" Mrs. Cohen asked finally.

Lisa nodded and sent the letter back up the table. She had wanted to wait, to be alone, but she knew instinctively that she must share the news, good or bad, with everyone. This was her family, they had helped her through it—this was their answer also.

Mrs. Cohen opened the letter with a clean knife, to preserve it, if need be, for posterity. She unfolded the thick, elegant stationery and read: "The Associated Board of the London Royal Academy of Music is"—here Mrs. Cohen paused to take a breath—"pleased to inform Miss Lisa Jura that . . ."

There was a scream at the end of the table from a young boy, who had a hand slapped over his mouth quickly, so the rest of the glowing faces at the table could hear the end of the sentence.

". . . she has been accepted into the scholarship program for the study of the pianoforte. Please report—"

A tumult as loud as any of the octaves from the end of the ballade broke out at the table. Lisa was swarmed and enveloped by kisses, hugs, and thumbs-up signs, and those who couldn't get close enough to give one started to clap. One boy began to whistle "God Save the King," while another yelled, "Soon we'll have to pay to hear her!" Lisa was a hero, and the children of Willesden Lane desperately needed a victory.

Everyone insisted that Lisa play them something from the audition, so the entire hostel crowded down the stairs to hear the *presto con fuoco* ending of the ballade. Hans, Gunter, and Gina put their arms around one another, swaying back and forth, savoring the payoff of their months of hard work. Even Aaron's absence could not mar Lisa's joy on this wonderful evening.

After the finale, Mrs. Glazer called them up for the special dessert she had made in secret (hoping that the news of the letter would be good). "Gingerbread for all," she announced, and the stampede began.

Mrs. Cohen stayed behind smiling; Lisa came up to her and put her arms around the matron. "I never would have even known about the audition if it weren't for you. How can I ever thank you?"

"You have thanked me. You've brought honor to this house," Mrs. Cohen replied.

"It's wonderful to see everyone so excited," Lisa answered shyly.

"Of course they're excited," the matron said. "We all need to dream, and tonight, everyone is living their dream through you."

To add to Lisa's euphoria, Aaron was released the following week from detention camp. He showed up at 243 Willesden to help celebrate Lisa's triumph.

"Where are you taking me?" Lisa demanded in that flirtatious tone Aaron loved.

"We're going to celebrate, and that's all I'm saying," was his answer.

Lisa ran upstairs, putting on her new pleated skirt and a chic blue blouse, topped by a stylish felt hat, and met him in the foyer. He whistled his approval, and off they went.

They jumped on a double-decker bus and hurried up the stairs to the top, huddling together in the cold, in order to appreciate the magnificent view from the open deck. The bus weaved its way past Buckingham Palace, down Oxford Street, and south toward the Thames. Each time Lisa insisted on knowing where they were going, Aaron merely laughed. They were having so much fun, they almost missed their stop—the Parliament building, or what was left of it after the bombing.

"What are we doing here?" Lisa asked, somewhat disappointed.

"Just wait, you'll see."

They waited for many cold minutes, as Aaron lit cigarette after cigarette, looking at his watch nervously.

"This better be good!" she teased, blowing a breath of frosty air at him.

Finally an old gentleman arrived and waved. "Hello, Mr. Lewin!" he said, shaking Aaron's hand. "Let's go!"

The man unlocked a nondescript door and ushered them into a hallway leading to some narrow stairs.

"Come on, hurry up!" Aaron said, and they followed the man up and up the stairs.

"Are we there yet?"

"Keep climbing! You'll just have to trust me," Aaron said, holding her hand tightly.

She followed him into the darkness of the winding stairwell.

When they reached the top, Lisa was blinded by the bright sunlight shooting through an open tower. Then she saw it—a giant clock with its inner workings and huge bells.

"It's Big Ben!" Aaron exclaimed.

"I can't believe it!" Lisa cried delightedly.

"Come on . . . look over here," Aaron said, pointing. "And here! Look!"

They were high above London, and the City stretched out below them, the House of Commons, the great dome of St. Paul, and the crowded winding streets. The Thames

215

flowed peacefully and disappeared into the distance. Lisa slipped her hand into Aaron's, but instead of taking it, he wrapped his arms around her, enveloping her in a kiss.

Then they stood, speechless, staring at the great panorama before them. The war, the bombs, and the destruction seemed to disappear, too.

At that moment, Lisa dared to have hope. Hope that the war could be won, hope that she'd see her family again, and hope that her dreams could come true. She could study! And if she studied hard enough, she could become what she had always dreamed—a concert pianist.

As she stared at the thousands of buildings and homes laid out before her, she imagined she was staring at a thousand faces—the faces in a concert hall—the faces in the daydream she used to have on the streetcar in Vienna. She allowed herself again to imagine the elegantly dressed audience waiting for her to begin. She could hear the hush and feel the anticipation as she sat in front of the nine-foot grand piano and began. Why couldn't it be so?

When she came out of her reverie and looked at Aaron, she saw he was also dreaming of faraway things. But he wasn't staring at the horizon, he was looking down at a group of British soldiers gathered beneath Big Ben's tower.

21

$\mathcal{T}$HE REAPPEARANCE of the crocuses in the spring of 1943 meant that another year had passed, but Lisa had barely noticed, she was so absorbed in her new studies. She hardly had time to read the corner chalkboard, which was plastered with encouraging headlines like ALLIES ENTER NAPLES and KIEV LIBERATED!

The Royal Academy of Music had proved as exciting as she had hoped and as demanding as she had anticipated. Theory classes, history classes, elements of orchestration— Lisa loved them all.

In the fall of 1942, her first year, she had been assigned a "master teacher" and was surprised when she opened the door to the small studio to find that it was the same small lady who had been on the jury at the audition. Her name was Mabel Floyd, a teacher with a very distinguished reputation.

Mrs. Floyd had greeted her warmly, giving Lisa great assurances about her talent (calling her a "diamond in the rough"), then launched into a first lesson where she corrected almost everything about Lisa's playing.

In the entire first hour of that first lesson, she did nothing but go over and over and over the first two pages of Chopin's ballade.

"Why did you put the space there, Lisa? Listen . . . it continues . . . it's a question, then an answer . . . keep going, Lisa! . . . That's right, it's driving now! Don't stop! . . . There! Wonderful, Lisa!"

That day Lisa walked home with Mabel Floyd's parting words ringing in her ears: "We have a lot of work to do!"

She couldn't wait to tell Hans all about it. "Can you believe it? One hour on two pages! At first, I thought she was going to be so reserved, this little British lady. But do you know what she did? She started singing the phrases before I played them. You should have seen her waving her arms all around, like she was conducting!"

Then Lisa sat at the piano: "Listen to this," she said, playing the new phrasing of the Chopin.

Hans listened carefully, smiling in appreciation. "Ah! Now you're sounding like Rubinstein!"

"You said I sounded like Rubinstein before," she shouted, above her playing.

"I was fibbing," he said, laughing.

She stopped, grabbed the music, and beat him playfully on the head.

That first year brought many other changes in Lisa's life. After a long struggle, Johnny had died, leaving a hole in the heart of the hostel. Lisa was devastated—she had really thought her friend would pull through, but his internal injuries were more severe than any of them had known. She missed him terribly.

To add to her loneliness, Aaron enlisted in the Auxiliary Military Pioneer Corps as a paratrooper. After having seen the look in his eyes as he watched the soldiers from the tower of Big Ben, Lisa knew his announcement should have come as no surprise—how long could he bear looking at the parade of heroes and not feel left behind?

At first she was excited, visualizing a war hero for a boyfriend. "Ooh, look at you, handsome!" Lisa said when Aaron first appeared in his neatly pressed uniform, having returned from training camp.

But when Lisa had to face the reality of their impending separation, she was distraught. On the night before he was to ship out, he came to the hostel to say good-bye, Mrs. Cohen kindly lending them her room for a few private hours to say good-bye.

When the evening was over, Aaron came into the living room and shook everyone's hands. It was especially hard for Gunter to see him go; he was feeling guilty for not having enlisted himself. But Gina consoled him by reminding him of his recent decision to dedicate himself to his studies. Gunter had decided to become a doctor, even though he knew it would be a struggle, since he was only now being given the opportunity to attend middle school.

Lisa was crying so hard that she couldn't leave Mrs. Cohen's room for the final glimpse of him going out the door.

At first she wrote him every day, then every week, but then she grew so busy that she wrote just once a fortnight. Aaron had done the same, as he was swept up in the life of the regiment and the hardships of the parachute division. In the beginning his letters were detailed and enthusiastic, but after his first combat experience, they became more guarded; Lisa tried to read between the lines. What was it like? What had he seen? She didn't want to imagine.

When the weather got warmer, Mrs. Cohen had the children plant the year's Victory garden—tomatoes, green beans and cucumbers. The younger children were given responsibility for the newest innovation—a backyard flock of laying hens.

"Eggs! I'd forgotten what they looked like," Mrs. Glazer said, marveling when the first one dropped.

The summer of 1943 brought the glorious news that, after a year of begging, the Bateses finally agreed that it was safe enough to allow Sonia to come and visit with her older sister in London.

Lisa met Sonia at the train and enveloped her in an enormous hug. She was surprised to see that Sonia was still thin and small for her sixteen years. "Are you getting enough to eat out in the country?" she asked anxiously.

"It's not like Mama's cooking, but don't worry, I'm trying to eat as much as I can." Not satisfied by this response, Lisa devoted most of the weekend they spent together to plying Sonia with whatever extra portions she could sneak from the kitchen.

Lisa took Sonia to all of her favorite spots in her new city: At Buckingham Palace they strained for a glimpse of the princess. Lisa wanted to show Sonia the tube but was unable to get her to ride the trains; the younger girl balked at entering the frightening hole in the ground, and no amount of convincing could persuade her. Giving up, Lisa suggested the double-decker bus, which they rode happily for hours before getting off to feed the pigeons in Trafalgar Square.

When they walked past Big Ben, Lisa confided that she

had been kissed on top of the bell tower. Sonia's eyes widened at her sister's brazen behavior, but Lisa told her that soon she, too, would meet a boy, and then she would understand.

The night was more difficult; Sonia cried out for their mother in her sleep, and asked, tearily, in the morning, when Lisa thought they would see their parents and Rosie again.

"I don't know," Lisa began, but seeing Sonia's mournful expression, she added, "I'm sure it will be soon."

Despite the rough moments, it was a wonderful visit, and both sisters were distraught on Sunday afternoon when it was time to part once again. They vowed to keep writing often, especially if either heard any news of the family.

Just a few weeks after Sonia's visit, Lisa got a short letter from Leo's cousin in Mexico. While letters from Austria had stopped completely, occasionally they still slipped in from other places. Lisa ripped open this letter and scanned it quickly for news.

"Still haven't heard from Leo or Rosie, but we did get news that most all Jews from Vienna have now been deported to detention camps in Poland, near Lodz, we think. We have tried desperately to get word about our aunts and uncles there, but there are few ways to communicate from here in Mexico. Do you have better sources for information over there? Please write us if you hear anything at all."

In panic, Lisa brought this letter to the Bloomsbury House, but neither they, nor the Jewish Refugee Agency, nor anyone else, could answer their frantic appeals. All letters came back stamped "Undeliverable," and every attempt Lisa and the others at the hostel made to contact their parents was unsuccessful.

* * *

Lisa struggled to maintain a degree of normalcy in her life. Her routine was hard; she awoke early and worked the first shift at the factory. By 1943, Platz & Sons was making military accessories—duffel bags, backpacks, mudguards, camouflage, all sewn from heavy green canvas. The work was harder than before, and Lisa's tired fingers began to feel the strain from the difficult, repetitive work of pushing yard after yard of heavy canvas under the presser foot of the sewing machine.

Then came her afternoon classes at the school of music, followed by the hours of practicing necessary to keep Mrs. Floyd happy. Because she was always working, she had no time to make friends with the other students and envied those she saw lounging and chatting in the halls, seemingly without a care in the world. She told herself that someday the hard work would pay off; she knew her mother would be proud of her.

On occasion, she, Hans, and Mrs. Cohen would go to the venerable Royal Albert Hall, with free tickets courtesy of Bloomsbury House. Lisa listened in rapture to the likes of pianist Clifford Curzon and the conducting of Sir John Barbirolli and was enthralled to see her idol, Myra Hess, play once again.

The centerpiece of her week was her lesson with Mabel Floyd. After faithfully practicing all that she had been assigned, she would appear enthusiastically at the master teacher's studio at three-thirty on Thursdays.

"No, no, no," Mrs. Floyd interrupted Lisa after just a few beats. "A trill is something light! Think of fairy dust, the tinkling of little bells. This sounds like a parade of army boots."

Lisa rubbed the painful muscles of her right forearm hurriedly and began again. The same results.

"No, no, try it from the beginning, please."

Again Lisa rubbed her arm before beginning.

"Is your arm bothering you, dear?" the teacher asked.

"No, it's all right. Just a little sore," Lisa answered, inadvertently rubbing it again.

"Maybe you're practicing too hard," Mrs. Floyd said, suddenly concerned. "How many hours do you practice every day?"

"Three," Lisa responded.

"Hmm, that sounds right. But let's work with the left hand for a while, give the right one a rest, shall we? Why don't you turn to that problem spot on page twelve."

As she flipped the pages, the discerning teacher noticed the worry in her pupil's eyes.

"Is there something else you need to tell me, dear?" she asked with concern.

Lisa had been reluctant to talk about her factory job with Mrs. Floyd, but finally she described her arduous work. The teacher had found out very little about her student; she knew only that she was a refugee and that she lived in a hostel, but she hadn't known the details about the rigors of the assembly line.

"My, my, we'll have to do something about that," was her brisk response. Saying no more about it, she gathered up Lisa's music and handed it to her. "Go home and get some rest. I'll see you next week. There will be no assignment."

At the end of the next lesson Mrs. Floyd handed Lisa a letter, handwritten in bold, black ink, on the embossed stationery of the Royal Academy.

"Take this to the Howard Hotel, the address is inside. They are looking for a pianist to entertain the soldiers. I believe the pay is reasonable and the work will be much more suitable."

Lisa drew in her breath—a little gasp of delight. "Oh, thank you! Thank you, Mrs. Floyd."

"And I'm sure you will, ah, take care to be, how do the French say it? *Sage*."

Lisa thought she saw the feisty woman wink, but it was so fast that she might have imagined it.

She floated several inches off the pavement all the way to the Howard Hotel, where she presented the letter to the manager, was shown the piano in the lounge adjacent to the bar, and was told she could begin the following week.

The next day at the factory was difficult; Lisa dreaded good-byes. She sat, teary eyed, as she was presented with a camouflage backpack that had been autographed by all the ladies on her floor. "Wishing you the best of luck, Love Lois, Doris, Deirdre, Rachel, Louise, et al."

Mr. Dimble said, "We're sorry to lose you, but good luck in show business." Lisa laughed and thanked him with a kiss on the cheek that made the poor man blush.

The farewell to Mrs. McRae was the hardest. "I'll be reading the newspapers, searching for your name, Lisa. I'll be reading the arts section! Won't that set them a-titterin'." They hugged, and with no further cere-mony Lisa left the life of the factory behind.

22

*T*HE HOWARD HOTEL was a bustling night spot in the West End of London, with a large restaurant, a small ballroom with swing dances on Saturday nights, and "entertainment in the lounge" the other six nights a week. Lisa posed for a photograph that was placed on an easel in the foyer: "In the Oak Room, Lisa Jura, at the Piano."

She had explained her classical training and lack of "popular repertoire" to the enormously busy manager.

"Fine, fine, fine, don't worry! You're very pretty, that's the main thing," he said, returning to his inventory of the glasses and bottles behind the bar.

The hotel atmosphere took some getting used to—the chatter and laughter, the clinking of glasses, the occasional brawl. But Lisa was happy and grateful, not only to be playing music, but to feel a part of the sophisticated beat of London.

The City was crawling with soldiers on leave—the Yanks, the Free French, and the Royal Navy, Air Force, and Army. Uniforms were as ubiquitous as civilian clothes, and it seemed that as many women wore them as men.

Gina was green with envy, but she rose above her feelings to help Lisa get ready for the first night. Lisa floated into the beauty salon, where her friend had stayed late to curl, swirl, and wrap her hair in the latest fashion. A touch of bright red lipstick, and off she went.

The first night, she chose the liveliest of Chopin's mazurkas and several of Mendelssohn's songs without words. She learned fast to avoid Bach and Beethoven. The crowd was appreciative, and so was the manager when he saw the patrons moving from the restaurant to the lounge to order additional drinks.

"Play 'Peg o' My Heart'!" someone yelled. "No, play 'I'll be Seeing You'!"

Lisa smiled and tried to be charming, but she realized immediately that she had better find some new music. The next day, reveling in the wonder of having a free morning, she shopped near Tottenham Court for the favorite tunes of the day.

Her training in sight-reading really paid off, and soon the entire room was singing along with Lisa's spirited versions of the wartime hit parade. She played "We'll Meet Again" and "I'm Gonna Get Lit Up (When the Lights Go Up in London)" and "When They Sound the Last 'All Clear.'"

More and more Americans were coming in, the overflow from the famous Rainbow Corners dance hall up the street, where Count Basie and Woody Herman blasted the big band sound to frenzied dancers leaping to the jitterbug. The Yanks loved it when she played "Praise the Lord and Pass the Ammunition" and yelled out for "Deep in the Heart of Texas." There was always some outgoing type who led the crowd in singing along, cheering loudly at the end of each favorite.

Truth be told, one of the things Lisa loved best about the job was being the center of attention. She was now nineteen; her hair was bobbed, there was a charming sway in her walk, and flirtatiousness was in her blood. The soldiers were young and oh, so handsome, and she was the center of this small universe in the lounge of the Howard Hotel. Mash notes were a nightly occurrence. "Would the beautiful lady with the red hair care to join me for our own Hungarian rhapsody? Squadron leader Lou 'Lucky' McGuire."

Sometimes, when she saw a soldier in an RAF uniform, she would think of Aaron, although more with nostalgia than with the sting of longing she had first felt at their parting. But her worry about him intensified after the hostel received a telegram from the War Department advising them that Paul Goldschmidt had died. The telegram was addressed to Mrs. Cohen, whose name had been filled in under "Mother." Mrs. Cohen passed the telegram around the quiet dinner table, and saddened fingers touched the words *valiantly gave his life in service . . .*

Mrs. Glazer led the recitation of the kaddish: "May God remember the soul of Paul Goldschmidt who has gone to his eternal home. . . ."

Paul's death was a blow to Lisa, not only because she missed his sunny smile but because it brought home the reality of the danger Aaron faced. The next day, she went to a small storefront shop that she had often passed in Cavendish Square, where she had seen the sign "Star Sound Studios—Send greetings to your loved ones far away!"

Even though the man was impressed by Lisa's rendition of Liszt's romantic *Liebesträume*, adjusting the dials of the huge machine that cut the grooves into the 78 rpm gramophone record, he still charged the full two pounds for the service. She left him the address of the paratroops division headquarters and inscribed the gold-and-white label in the center "Dear Aaron, with all my love, Lisa."

As time went by it became easier to put thoughts of Aaron aside as night after night Lisa entered this sophisticated new world. She loved her new job, and what she loved most about it was the fellowship, the soldiers and bomb-weary Londoners who were looking for a haven of friendly camaraderie as much as she was.

But how many times could she play "Peg o' My Heart" without feeling starved for the depth and beauty of the great composers? So it was with renewed enthusiasm that she redoubled her practicing and went to her weekly lesson with Mabel Floyd.

"Architecture!" the master teacher said for what seemed like the hundredth time. "You must envision the whole of the piece, not just these little segments I hear. Try the last section again, please."

And once again Lisa played the offending section while Mrs. Floyd listened intently.

"Shh! Let the melody build, don't give it all away at the start," she said, starting to sing the beautiful melody, raising and lowering the volume of her voice as Lisa approached the climactic moments. "That's it! Hear that? It's the answer to the question on the other page. . . . Now keep it going! . . . Don't stop there! . . . That's right, Lisa! Listen to the response!"

Eyes shining, Lisa began building to the thunderous

conclusion. She was beginning to think she'd make it this time.

"No, no, no!" Mrs. Floyd said, stopping her once again. "You've lost the rhythm. If the pattern of the left hand becomes erratic, the architecture is lost! Once again, now."

By the end of a lesson, the pages of Lisa's music were covered by arrows, circles, and annotations of all descriptions. It was hard work, but Lisa emerged from the studio filled with exhilaration.

Gina usually got back to the hostel from the beauty parlor around the time Lisa was putting the finishing touches on her makeup, readying herself for her evening of glamour on the West End. Recently her smiles and compliments at Lisa's elegant new clothing had dried up and were replaced by a coolness that was subtle but unmistakable.

One Friday night, when Lisa was trying on an expensive new jacket (which had cost a week's salary and used up her remaining allotment of sixteen clothing ration coupons), Gina walked in, put her purse on the bed, and frowned.

"Isn't it dreamy?" Lisa asked, anxious for her friend's approval of the tailored masterpiece.

"The color is awful on you," she answered. "It's totally wrong for a redhead." Gina turned and walked downstairs for dinner.

Lisa surveyed herself again in the mirror, turning nervously. She had paid a lot of money for this jacket! Suddenly, from the top bunk across the room, came the voice of Edith from over the pages of her movie magazine.

"It looks just fine, don't listen to her."

"I wish she'd just be nice for once!" Lisa said angrily.

"Don't you see what she wants, silly?" said Edith.

"What?" Lisa asked, genuinely not having a clue.

229

"She wants you to take her with you," came the advice from her usually silent roommate.

It was so simple, Lisa couldn't imagine why she hadn't thought of it before.

Lisa was thrilled at the prospect of sharing the evening at the lounge with her best friend and delighted that Gina had accepted her invitation. She was also amazed that Gunter had let Gina come without him; he'd become a real bore since he'd begun to study so hard.

"Ooh, it's a good thing the stick-in-the-mud isn't coming! Wait until you see all the Yanks!" said Lisa as the two young women hurried up Shaftsbury Street.

At first Gina sat alone at her own table, but she was soon mobbed by soldiers looking for a date. She bantered and chatted with the calm confidence of a woman who knows her heart is already taken.

Lisa played a moving rendition of "Deep Purple," which momentarily stopped the chatter in the crowded room. At the end of it, she stood up to acknowledge the applause, and looked over in Gina's direction, announcing loudly: "That was dedicated to my best friend."

Gina took a little bow, and a group of American sailors rushed over to the pretty girl, saying, "Let me buy you a drink to celebrate!"

"Why not?" Gina smiled.

"'Red River Valley'!" one of the sailors called out, and Lisa launched into the simple tune. After a few bars, he began to sing. "From this valley they say you are going . . . We will miss your bright eyes and sweet smile . . ." He had a haunting tenor voice, and the raucous crowd quieted immediately. He sang so beautifully that Lisa stopped playing and let him finish a capella.

230

"So remember the Red River Valley . . . And the cowboy who loved you so true. . . ."

When he finished, there were tears in the eyes of many soldiers who were thinking mournfully of the beautiful girls back home.

At the end of the evening, Gina gathered up her purse and coat and walked over to Lisa. "I'm coming back every Friday night, no matter what you-know-who thinks. It's too much fun to miss!"

One night, Lisa glanced out at the faces of the soldiers in the room and did a double take. For there was Aaron, completely unexpected, but, judging from the quickening of her pulse, more welcome than she had realized. She immediately stopped the piece she was playing, jumped up, threw her arms around him, and gave him a kiss. The crowd burst into cheers and catcalls, which then turned into the rhythmic clapping whose message was unmistakable: Get back to the piano!

"Sit right there! I'll join you at the break!" Lisa said excitedly, then sat back down and launched into a heartfelt rendition of the *Liebesträume*, just for him.

Several inebriated flyboys nearby saw the fond looks she was throwing Aaron and whistled their approval.

When at last her work was done, she hurried to his table, where he sat alone in front of several emptied glasses.

"How about this place? Pretty fancy, don't you think?" she said, pulling out a cigarette. Saying nothing, Aaron leaned forward and lit it with his lighter.

"Don't look at me like that, you smoke, too! So, what do you think?" she continued with excitement.

"You played even more beautifully than your record-ing."

"Oh, you got it!" Lisa cried out happily.

"Yes, thank you."

A soldier approached Lisa, offering to buy her a drink, but she refused politely, following Aaron's eyes as he watched the handsome soldiers all around her.

"Now, don't be jealous. It's just a job."

Aaron smiled wryly, and blew smoke rings into the air.

"So, tell me everything!" she begged.

"You first."

Lisa chattered about the hostel and the Howard Hotel, but the more she went on, the more she realized she was looking at a changed Aaron. Where was his devilish swag-ger? He seemed so remote. She waited until he finished his drink, then she stood up, grabbing his hand. "Come on! Let's go for a walk. I see too much of this hotel already."

They walked slowly through the narrow cobblestone streets near Covent Garden, then meandered west up the wider avenues heading for Hyde Park. The streets were dark and deserted except for the occasional giggling cou-ple, hurrying back to their homes or to barracks after a late-night rendezvous.

The gates to Hyde Park, where Lisa and Aaron had walked so often before, were locked. The antiaircraft guns stood as silent sentries behind the iron fence. They could make out the red glow of lit cigarettes near the huge guns, then staring closer, saw gunnery sergeants peering through binoculars into the clear, starry sky.

"Tell me about it, Aaron, what is it like?" Lisa asked gently, putting her arm on his shoulder.

In a monotone, he spoke about his regiment and his

training. He had joined a parachute company in the 1st Airborne Division and had trained in a secret location. When he described the sensations of jumping out of a plane, he became briefly animated, like the Aaron she remembered. Then he fell silent again, just walking slowly, as though he had no destination.

Lisa took his hand but didn't feel any warmth from it; his coldness frightened her. The closer she clung to him, the more distanced she felt.

She wondered many things that she was afraid to ask. Were all soldiers like this? Was this what war did? Did it ruin everything? Where was the charming suitor who had whistled the Grieg in her ear? Where was the hurt but gentle boy who had watched his father walk out of the house, never to return.

"What was it like when you landed someplace?" she asked.

"You don't want to know," he answered, lighting two cigarettes and giving her one.

"Were you scared?"

"Of course, what do you think?"

"I don't know. That's why I'm asking. I want you to talk to me," she begged.

Aaron stayed stubbornly silent, and finally, Lisa stopped asking questions. After a while, he stopped abruptly, cocking his head toward the sky.

"What is it?" Lisa asked, alarmed.

"Shh," he answered, standing perfectly still. Suddenly, before she could hear the sound that Aaron heard, the night was broken with the wail of air-raid sirens.

"It's a V-2, hurry!" He took her hand and they ran together toward the underground station at Marble Arch. A wave of people rushed frantically from their blacked-out apartments and onto the sidewalks, carrying books, blankets, and hastily grabbed snacks. Aaron and Lisa ran after them, joining the hurried stream of Londoners running down the stairs into the safety of the tubes.

Down and down they went; Lisa stopped counting how many flights, grateful to be so deeply hidden from the approach of the German buzz bombs. When they arrived at the lowest floor, the cold tiled platforms were already covered by rows of sleeping bodies; these were the early birds, who had taken to spending every night in the tubes, not waiting for the sirens.

People were everywhere—on the escalators, on the stairs, draped over benches and chairs. The more organized families had brought cots and blankets; the others lay huddled next to strangers for warmth. Lisa's mouth dropped at the sight of all the people; she had heard about these places, but had never been caught out at night in an air raid before.

With sleepy eyes, the tightly packed masses readjusted themselves to make room for the latecomers. Aaron found a wall to lean against, and the family next to them moved over a few inches with a nod of respect to his uniform. He took off his jacket and spread it underneath Lisa to shield her from the cold.

They were too far underground to hear the whine of the bombers, but every few minutes the ceiling gave off a layer of dirt and dust, shaken loose by the explosions topside.

Aaron leaned his head against the dirty, cement wall and stared at the sooty Londoners around him. "People are a sorry lot, aren't they? We're nothing but canon fodder," his voice drifted off again into silence.

Lisa leaned her head on his shoulder and stared at the sleeping children next to them. An angelic two-year-old slept next to her leg, and as he tossed and turned, he yanked his blanket off, exposing his little pink legs. She pulled it back over him and realized as she did that tears were streaming from her eyes. She closed them and buried her face deeply into Aaron's shoulder.

The all clear siren sounded several hours later and they dusted themselves off, making their way toward Willesden Lane. Overcome with exhaustion, Aaron and Lisa stood silently for a long moment in front of the hostel, watching the first light of dawn glowing in the eastern sky.

When they kissed good-bye, Lisa held him tightly, transported for a moment to the feelings she had the night when he first kissed her outside Mrs. Canfield's house. The tighter she clung, the more she felt confused. Were these feelings merely the ghosts of her feelings from the past, or did she truly still care for him?

When she finally let go, Aaron smiled mysteriously and picked up his satchel.

"I'll write you when I arrive," he said, and walked slowly down the road.

She watched until he turned the corner and was sure she heard him whistling the first few bars of the Grieg.

"Lisa! Thank God!" Gina shouted when she saw Lisa tiptoe into the bedroom a few minutes later. "We were worried sick! Where were you?"

"I was caught in an air raid," Lisa answered, in no mood to share confidences. "I had to spend the night in the underground."

"We were really worried, they said a rocket fell near the hotel."

Lisa said nothing as she put on her warm flannel nightgown and climbed into bed.

"Can I tell you something?" Gina asked, her voice filled with excitement.

Lisa waited silently, still lost in her upsetting thoughts.

"Gunter and I are engaged, look!" Gina exclaimed, holding out her left hand. There was a simple gold ring on her finger. "This is just temporary," she said, "until he can afford the real one. He promised someday he'll buy me a diamond. You have to promise you'll play at our wedding! Promise?"

"Of course," Lisa answered smiling, disguising her sadness.

"Oh, thank you, thank you! I can't begin to tell you how excited I am," Gina went on, detailing the plans from beginning to end.

Lisa listened but her mind kept wandering to Aaron, trying to picture the images of happier times. Maybe when the war is over, he will change back into the Aaron I love, she told herself.

The next day, she felt grateful to escape her dark thoughts and return to her work entertaining the cheerful, raucous soldiers at the Howard Hotel.

23

$\mathcal{B}$Y 1944, the war was finally going their way. The Allies were heading for Rome and Russia had liberated Odessa. London was now crawling with soldiers—more than ever before—they were on the streets, in the theaters, and packed in, standing room only, at the Howard Hotel. Lisa reveled in the attention of the soldiers—the feeling that the war's tide was turning in their favor buoyed their spirits and led to an increase in mash notes and free drinks sent her way.

Tonight, Lisa was wearing a long gray dress with a deep V and a triple strand of fake pearls that looked almost like the real thing. She was looking her sophisticated best and decided to use the opportunity of such a large crowd to try out the Rachmaninoff prelude she had just learned in preparation for her year-end recital.

The mysterious aura of the Rachmaninoff matched the mood of expectation. Leaves had been canceled abruptly; most of the soldiers knew they would be back on ships and planes the next day. The hush in the lounge was deeper than usual; there were none of the customary interruptions by the more inebriated soldiers at the bar. When Lisa played the powerful ending, several soldiers gathered around the piano to watch the bravura of her flying octaves.

After the applause, three soldiers approached, led by a lieutenant, carrying a carnation. He stepped forward and said:

"Mademoiselle! There is a gentleman who wants to meet you." The soldier had such a strong French accent and such charming determination that Lisa didn't feel the least bit like saying no. Besides, it was time for her break.

She followed them back to a table, where a tall man, with compelling dark brown eyes and a wonderfully direct expression stood up immediately. He held out his hand and she took it, assuming he wanted to shake, but he raised it to his lips gracefully and kissed it instead.

"*C'était magnifique! Que vous êtes magnifique!*"

"I'm sorry, I don't speak French," Lisa said. Seeing his puzzled look, she tried to mime the words and threw her hands in the air in a playful shrug of defeat.

"Rachmaninoff!" he said, cupping both hands over his heart.

"Ah, so you know!" She beamed at him.

Then it was his turn to throw his hands in the air.

"You don't speak any English?" Lisa asked.

"His English is terrible," said his friend, speaking for him. "But he's really a smart fellow, underneath."

"*Czy ty mowiszi?*"

"He's asking if you speak Polish. He's from Lomja, but he's in the Resistance, fighting for the Free French. He's our captain."

"No Polish," Lisa said, laughing.

"*Voulez-vous du Cointreau?*" he asked, offering a small glass filled with the golden liqueur.

She shook her head. "No, thank you."

The captain then said something in a deep voice to his lieutenant, who turned to Lisa and translated.

"He says to tell you that you are the most beautiful woman he has ever seen."

Lisa had heard this quite a bit at the Howard Hotel from soldiers who had been away from their girlfriends too long, never letting it go to her head. But this time, intrigued by the aura of strength about the French captain, she found herself believing it, just a little.

Suddenly she became aware of the time. Realizing she'd been chatting for half an hour—twice her standard break—she excused herself, thanked them for their compliments, and went back to the piano, where she gave in to the audience's irrepressible desire to hear "Peg o' My Heart" yet another agonizing time.

When it came near to the eleven o'clock closing—the time most soldiers had to get back to barracks—she looked up and saw, through the thinning crowd, that the Resistance soldier was still there. He was now sitting alone at the table, with his eyes trained firmly on Lisa. When she finished the last chord, he made his way through the jumble of men and women to the piano.

"Beau-ti-ful," he said, once again putting his hands over his heart.

His friend came through the crowd right behind him, tapping his watch. The captain pulled out his calling card and handed it to Lisa, looking in her eyes and saying a few words in French.

The lieutenant translated: "He says you must promise to

invite him if ever you give a concert. He says, no matter where he is, he will come."

The next night, there was an unusual emptiness at the Howard Hotel. Lisa played a few songs for the bartender and the waitresses and the ten or so soldiers who milled about with pints of lager. The manager soon told her to take the night off.

On her way back home, she looked up at the sky and saw wave after wave of transport planes flying overhead. The Allied invasion of Europe had begun.

Lisa had been working toward the final, end-of-term recital that students gave in late June to the faculty and students of the Royal Academy of Music.

She arrived at her lesson with Mrs. Floyd and played through the pieces in a run-through for the upcoming event. Mrs. Floyd clapped appreciatively at the end, and Lisa took out her pencil and prepared to mark the music as usual with the new round of critiques. To her surprise, the teacher asked her to put her pencil away.

"Lisa, I don't have any notes today. It is time to trust yourself; you are ready to soar!"

After so many lessons where she had heard her playing dissected and analyzed, this was wonderful news. Lisa would go to this recital and finally play "what was in her heart."

"One more thing," Mrs. Floyd said with a twinkle in her eye.

Lisa waited.

"It's time to think about your debut."

Lisa was so stunned, she said nothing.

"Usually, a student's family helps toward the expenses of a debut, but because of your circumstances, the faculty has recommended that the academy help in the arrangements."

Lisa remained speechless.

"That is, if you would like a debut," Mrs. Floyd said, teasing.

Lisa leapt from her seat, crying, "Of course I would!" and wrapped her arms around her instructor in an exuberant, spontaneous hug. "I don't know how to thank you," Lisa said, genuinely honored.

"Oh, and one more thing. For the location of your debut . . . we are thinking of Wigmore Hall."

Wigmore Hall! It was incredible. The moment she had dreamed about all her life was finally within her grasp.

24

*T*HE JUNE recital had gone off without a hitch and Lisa settled into a summer and fall of choosing and preparing new repertoire for her debut. The Howard Hotel remained a popular night spot and now Gunter took to joining Gina for a weekly Friday-night visit.

As winter came, the battles in Europe raged even more intensely and it was decided to wait a season to rent Wigmore Hall for the debut. Rationing was severe and people's minds were on war, not music. January saw the Allies battling through a frozen Europe, taking back city after city from the Third Reich. Russia marched through Poland— first Warsaw, then Lodz—and the United States and Great Britain obliterated Dresden in a firestorm.

When she heard there was a battle raging for Vienna, Lisa went to the synagogue and said a special prayer. Would it be a firestorm too? Would her city disappear as Dresden had?

Through the avalanche of news, the children of Willesden Lane waited. Waited for letters, waited for word. Straining for news from the deportation camps, where they knew their parents were waiting—to be liberated.

Lisa tried mightily to center herself in the music and her practice, and Mrs. Floyd helped her perfect the repertoire for her debut. Her favorite new piece was the Polonaise in A-flat Major of Chopin—the *Heroic*—whose triumphal notes seemed a fitting tribute to what surely would be a great Allied victory. Even Lisa, who was always afraid to get her hopes up, allowed herself to believe the day was near.

"That's right, Lisa, keep it building, just like that. . . ." said Mrs. Floyd.

Lisa played the melody and accompanied it with the images in her mind. She vividly imagined the impending day of the reunion with her family. She played the chords with a boundless joy that summed up all her prayers and visions of that day. She saw her mother's smiling face and outstretched arms, her father's embrace, their weary faces smiling, their troubles lifted. She pounded the piano in joy, imagining Rosie's and Sonia's shouts of delight the day the three sisters would be united.

In the middle of a thunderous passage, the door to the studio flew open and two excited girls poked in their heads.

"Hurry up! Haven't you heard?"

Lisa lifted her hands from the keys, and when the ringing of the polonaise died away, they could hear the faraway bells—the pealing of the clock tower, of Big Ben! Then the sounds gathered momentum—and were joined by the bells of the churches all throughout London.

Lisa ran to the window; traffic had slowed to a crawl and people were running and shouting and jumping in the air.

Union Jacks sprouted from every window, and horns were honking wildly.

Lisa had never seen Mrs. Floyd move so fast, but there she was, leading a group of excited students lickety-split down the spiral staircase and into the streets, where they joined the growing crowd. They boarded a packed trolley for Buckingham Palace, which wove through a sea of revelers wearing paper hats and waving noisemakers. When the trolley could no longer move, they got out and were pushed the remaining blocks to the Mall, where Churchill himself was addressing the throng.

Lisa was awestruck. She had heard his broadcasts, seen him on the newsreels and in the newspapers—but here he was in person, the man whose words had given strength to everyone during the dark years. Here was the obstinate, beloved prime minister, waving to the assembled masses, homburg in hand.

"God bless you all. This is your victory!" he roared into the microphone.

The crowd roared back. "No! It is yours!"

"There we stood alone, did anyone want to give in?" the prime minister thundered, his words echoing across the vast expanse.

"No!" The crowd shouted again.

"Were we downhearted?"

"No!"

"In all our long history we have never seen a greater day than this," he said, waving his famous hat.

Then when it seemed the crowd could not get any more excited, the king and queen and the princesses appeared on the balcony, waving and saluting as the crowds cheered, and the bells redoubled their ringing.

Lisa looked at the upturned faces surrounding her and

was overtaken by a profound feeling of gratitude for Britain and its people. They had endured so much and with such good spirit. She was proud to be one of them. She, too, had endured.

When the speeches were over, people began to sing and dance as bands were hastily assembled on street corners and bonfires lit. Total strangers embraced one another as they jammed overflowing pubs. For the first time since the blackout had begun five years before, the streetlights flickered to life and giant searchlights crisscrossed the sky.

The war in Europe was over! Hitler was dead! The Allies had taken Berlin! The horror was over—at least for the millions and millions of British who had fought so proudly and suffered so much.

Staring at the unmitigated joy on people's faces, Lisa was suddenly overcome with a shiver of isolation and sadness. When would the war be over for her? Or for her friends at the hostel?

From the swirl of the crowd, Mrs. Floyd and the other students reappeared and invited Lisa to join them for a victory dinner.

"Oh, thank you so much," Lisa answered. "But I think maybe I should celebrate with the others at home," she said, suddenly not feeling at all in a celebratory mood.

"Are you sure?" her teacher yelled above the noisy crowd.

Lisa nodded her head and waved good-bye as two of the students grabbed Mrs. Floyd by the hand, pushing the elegant English lady into a conga line that danced away from her. Lisa headed away from the raucous festivities.

The buses had stopped running, since the drivers had given up trying to navigate the crowded streets, so Lisa decided to walk home. She waded against a tide of well-wishers who flashed the V-for-Victory salute as they walked by. Gradually the crowd thinned, and with it, the sense of exhilaration and camaraderie. She walked faster and faster past rows of boarded-up buildings and shops—trudging forlornly over the bomb-scarred streets and past the destruction. When she came to her beloved Hyde Park she was buoyed temporarily to see that the swans had survived. She stood by the pond for a long moment, watching them swimming in gentle gliding motions over an eerily still pond. Beautiful things could survive, she told herself; she tried to have hope.

In the cold, dark stillness of the waters she superimposed an image of what she imagined would exist across the English Channel—a dark and silent Europe, battered and ruined, so far from her now. Her mind conjured up the streets of Vienna she'd left behind so long ago—and she saw for a moment the smiling faces of the beloved ones left behind. She thought she could hear their laughter the day of the ill-fated picnic on the balcony. Where were they now? Where were her mother and father and sister Rosie?

Chilled and lonely, she left the park and headed up the large avenue toward Edgware Road. More revelers ran by her, anxious to celebrate—their nightmare of waiting was over. But for Lisa and her fellow *Kinder* on Willesden Lane, the nightmare of waiting had just begun.

At first, there were just rumors. Unsubstantiated rumors, impossible rumors, which spread like wildfire through the already broken hearts of the Jewish community. Place names like Treblinka, Bergen-Belsen, Nordhausen, Auschwitz, and Theresienstadt were whispered from ear to ear.

Talk of mass graves, piles of bodies, piles of unspeakable obscenities. Photos leaked out of hollow-eyed inmates staring from behind barbed-wire fences, their fleshless, bony bodies hardly able to stand.

Lisa couldn't read most of the articles about it in the newspaper. She couldn't bear to hear it when she was told. She had known the terror of the Nazis, seen Kristallnacht, but never could she have imagined what had transpired, unreported, behind Nazi lines.

She couldn't practice, either, although sometimes she would play exercises and scales, comforted by the mindless repetition. It was difficult to go to her job at the Howard Hotel and watch the smiling people as they talked of their hopeful futures, but she needed the money and was grateful for the distraction.

Finally the Red Cross, the United Nations, and the U.S. Army began to post lists of concentration camp survivors as they were liberated, moved, and organized in camps for displaced persons.

Lisa flocked with the other desperate refugees to the agencies posting the lists. The pages were chaotic and disorganized, taped to walls in crowded hallways, often not dated, not alphabetized, put up as soon as beleaguered workers could type them, to help the frantic search of the heartbroken relatives.

She went every day to see if new lists had been compiled, going over and over the old ones with care. Seeing that there were no Juras on the list, Lisa looked for Leo's name. There were dozens of Schwartzes, but no Leos and no Rosies.

Rumor guided the search for lists. Gina would hear that new lists were at the United Nations Relief Agency, then someone else would hear that names were posted at the

U.S. Army Office, which oversaw the displaced persons camps, or at the World Jewish Congress offices, or in hastily printed Jewish newspapers.

Mr. Hardesty wandered through the halls and saw faces he recognized from the Kindertransport so many years earlier. He saw Lisa and greeted her with tender care. He looked at the crowded hallways, filled with some of the ten thousand *Kinder* who had been saved by their hurriedly organized train rescue. Ten thousand now seemed so few.

One day Gunter found his mother's name on the list from a displaced persons camp near Theresienstadt. Shaking with emotion, he spent the day writing hurried telegrams to make contact. When he returned to the hostel, he was so sensitive to the others' pain that he told only Gina about his news, feeling it was selfish to talk openly of his good fortune. But Mrs. Cohen heard and spread the word, feeling it important that what little joy there was should be shared.

During those first months of searching, Lisa would often lie on her bed and stare at her parents' pictures, placed reverently on her nightstand, and try hard to remember their faces. Their real features had long ago been replaced by the features she had memorized from the photographs. Sometimes, but only in a dream, she thought she could catch a glimpse of her mother's expression the night she had wiped the blood from her father's face on Kristallnacht. She had tried over and over to recapture it. And she could sometimes see the smile her mother gave her when they would play together at the piano after her lesson with Professor Isseles. Sometimes she was sure she caught a glimpse of it, though other times it seemed unbearably dim.

* * *

Yis'ga'dal v'yis'kadash—May the great Name of God be exalted. Nightly, the prayers at the synagogues chanted the names of the departed.

One weekend afternoon, a familiar figure walked through the front door of the hostel. It was Aaron Lewin, carrying his air force satchel and wearing the insignia of lieutenant.

Mrs. Cohen was the first to recognize him. "Aaron! How wonderful to see you. Come in, come in!" There was no hint of her former animosity. War had put such petty matters behind them.

"Is Lisa here?" he asked, direct as always.

"Yes, she's upstairs, please go on up."

"Aaron!" Lisa yelled, leaping off the bed. "It's so good to see you!" And it was good to see him again; he looked so mature, so sophisticated. She gave him a brief hug but the atmosphere between them was distant—she had gotten no letters from him for many months.

"I was worried about you! Are you all right?"

"Never better," he answered but his expression said the opposite. "This place looks like it needs some attention," he continued, glancing at the cracked glass of the window. "Maybe I should grab the toolbox."

Lisa smiled and led him to the kitchen to find the matron. She knew intuitively that Aaron needed time to get his bearings.

They spent the day together. Lisa watched as Aaron tackled the mechanical things that badly needed fixing. He worked in silence.

After lunch, Lisa felt it was time to broach the difficult

question she had been waiting all morning to ask. "Have you heard anything about your family, about your mother?"

"My mother is dead. So are my brothers," he answered, not adding any details.

"How?"

"I don't know. How would we ever know?"

"Then how are you sure they're dead?"

"We have to just assume it, don't we?" he said flatly, trying to shield himself from the pain of his words.

"How can you just 'assume' it?" she said, starting to get upset.

"Lisa, you must be realistic. I think it's time you faced it. What are the chances any of them survived?"

"Am I supposed to give up hope? Is that what you're saying?" Lisa asked trying to sound defiant. But her words came out halfhearted. It was her turn to be silent. She looked out the kitchen window at the gray sky and felt a leaden, numbing sadness. Could it be possible that she would never see her parents or Rosie again?

As the long summer afternoon was ending, Aaron asked Lisa to come with him into the back garden. They walked over the lush grass to the hedge that separated the hostel from the convent next door. Lisa's heart was still heavy from the terrible realizations that were beginning to wash over her.

Aaron had his back to her as he said, "I'll be leaving for New York. I've managed a visa for America."

"Oh," she said, with an involuntary gasp at the unexpected news.

Still facing away from her, he continued: "Will you come with me?"

Lisa was silent. Her world was fragmenting around her; she was facing the loss of everyone she held dear. Could she bear to lose Aaron even if she knew her feelings had changed? She didn't know if she had the strength to say no.

When Aaron turned around, he saw her deep in troubled thought and knew her answer.

A week later, Aaron came to the hostel before his final departure, bringing candies and cakes. Everyone was overjoyed, and no one asked him how he got them. He was trying to be positive and forward looking, fighting, as they all were, for a reason to go on. He had found his in the journey to America.

Lisa's reason? She didn't know. She could only stand sadly on the steps of the hostel, next to Gunter and Gina, and wave good-bye.

The Rachmaninoff Prelude in C-sharp Minor reached into the vast emptiness of Wigmore Hall. Professor Floyd arranged for Lisa to practice in the art deco auditorium where her concert would take place in two months' time.

Lisa worked through her program, playing flawlessly, but with a disquieting coldness that worried her teacher. Mrs. Floyd knew the unbearable pressures that her prized student was under. She had been following the terrible reports of the Jewish Holocaust in the newspapers, but she hoped a gentle prodding would keep her prized pupil on track.

From several rows back in the empty theater, she called. "Lisa, did you practice the things we spoke about last week?"

"A little bit, I'm sorry, not like I should have," Lisa answered, afraid to admit that she hadn't practiced at all.

"Let's not forget that the date is almost upon us. I don't want to frighten you, but the critics can be quite harsh on a new pianist. Ah, let's try the prelude from the *maestoso*, shall we?"

Lisa closed her eyes and began again, but there were no pictures or images to inspire her. She couldn't see the faces of the people she loved. She played on and tried to shield herself from the heartbreaking beauty of the music, which she knew her family, lost forever, would never share.

25

*G*INA AND GUNTER made a handsome bride and groom. Their big day had finally arrived and they sat with the rabbi in the living room of the hostel and signed the *ketubah*.

In spite of Mrs. Cohen's dedicated planning, the day had been hectic with last minute preparations. The older girls had swarmed into the kitchen, turning hoarded sugar and flour into kugel, Sacher torten, and an only moderately successful *apfelstrudel*. The boys, meanwhile, were frantically putting the finishing touches on the *chuppah* in the backyard.

The florist from the high street delivered the flowers with thirty minutes to spare. And last but not least, with a herculean effort, six of the strongest boys had lifted the piano and carried it out to the back lawn.

Lisa had put on her brightest face for the happy occasion, a feat made easier because finally, her sister Sonia had been allowed to move to London. She had moved into the hostel the week before. The war was over, and the city was safe, but even so the conscientious Bateses had called every day to see how their beloved charge was adjusting to her new life. Sonia was delighted to be near her older sister; most traces of her frightened demeanor had completely disappeared. The sisters had been put in charge of the wedding dress and had helped Gina to shop in the secondhand stores on the Edgeware Road until they found the perfect elegant lace gown.

Now, with ten minutes to spare, Gina had put her foot through the hem. The Jura sisters yelled for a needle and thread, and in no time, the beautiful bride was ready.

Rabbi Silverstein performed the ceremony, reciting the ancient prayers and asking the couple to exchange the traditional Jewish vows.

Yet for all the merriment that led up to it, the service itself was a somber occasion. Everyone was painfully aware of the enormity of the void in the group of gathered relatives and friends.

Gina's parents had died in Treblinka. Gunter's father had succumbed to a heart attack while being deported. Gone were Mrs. Cohen's entire family, as were Mrs. Glazer's . . . and so the list of the void went on down to the last orphan who stood watching. Only Gunter's mother had been on the "lists," and she was still in a hospital in a displaced persons camp near Theresienstadt.

Some of the "children" like Gina and Gunter were trying to move forward with their lives and had accepted the terrible news. But others still held out hope that at any moment, from out of the wreckage of Europe, their parents and siblings would miraculously appear. Lisa wavered between the two extremes.

When the vows were over, Gunter kissed his bride and

stepped on the champagne glass to cries of *"Mazel tov!"* Then the assembly of well-wishers clapped and the music began.

Although still in no mood to play, Lisa had agreed, out of a sense of duty, to perform the first movement of the Grieg piano concerto. As the notes of the first few bars floated into the warm outdoor air, Lisa couldn't help but think of Aaron. He had sent a congratulatory telegram from the *Île de France*, where he was on his way to a new life. Although her feelings for him were no longer romantic, Lisa missed his presence terribly.

She played the evocative concerto and thought of the images her mother had taught her, of the fjords, of Norway, of the placid, icy waters of Grieg's homeland. The images and their reverent mood helped to calm her overflowing emotions. She watched Gunter and Gina as she played, their love so radiantly displayed on their faces, and continued her musical tribute to their friendship—and to the friendship of all who were gathered here. So much was changing, the emotion was almost too much to bear. To keep from breaking down, she forced her thoughts back to the icy panoramas of the Grieg and managed to make it through the piece.

When she was finished, she got up to prepare a surprise.

"Please wait a moment, everyone," she said, and walked over to Hans and escorted him to the piano.

He played a beautiful rendition of "The Girl with the Flaxen Hair" by Debussy, which Lisa had been coaching him on for weeks. She had found a simple solace in being a teacher, and in truth, she hadn't known what else to do. The lessons paid off and made for a beautiful surprise, especially for Hans's mother, who broke down in tears.

Gunter then gave a toast to "all those missing today,"

making special mention of Paul and Johnny "King Kong." "May we remember the beauty of their gentle spirits and keep their memory in our hearts for the rest of our lives."

Feeling the pall that had been cast by Gunter's words, and not wanting the wedding day to turn somber, Mrs. Glazer hurried to bring out the cake. After the couple did a ceremonial cutting of the first piece, the bride rushed to open her presents, which were stacked neatly on the dining room table. Lisa waited patiently for Gina to open her gift, two silver candlesticks.

Then Gunter announced formally what they had all assumed, that he and Gina would be heading for New York as soon as his mother joined them, hopefully before the month was out. Lisa hugged her friends warmly, and was gripped by the sadness of another good-bye.

Children were arriving at the hostel from the displaced persons camps of Europe, where they had been brought from the hell of Bergen-Belsen, Auschwitz, and Dachau, and again there was a premium on space at Willesden Lane. Unlike the *Kinder* of 1939, these children had gaunt eyes that had seen things not even an adult could bear.

Mrs. Cohen had decided to stay on, having made her peace with losing the wealth and status of her past life in Berlin. She had found a calling in the difficult but rewarding job of matron.

The older *Kinder* were moving out to make room for younger children, and Lisa was among them. She was now twenty-one years old, and although it was hard for her to grasp, she had been in England for six years—many of them in this room she was now leaving.

It had been decided that Lisa would move to Mrs. Canfield's. Her son had been killed by a mortar shell while dressing a soldier's wounds and the matron had asked if Lisa would go live with the Quaker woman, insisting the company would do the grieving mother good. And remembering her generosity during the bombing of the hostel, Lisa was only too glad to repay the debt of kindness.

Sonia, now eighteen, would take over Lisa's bunk. Her sister wouldn't be under the same roof, but she would be right around the corner.

On the day of the move, Sonia watched as Lisa took down the black-and-white photo of Leslie Howard in *Gone with the Wind*, which was taped on the wall above the bed.

"Want me to leave this?" Lisa asked.

"Who is it?" said Sonia, staring at the blond heartthrob.

"Who is it? I guess I'll have to take you to the movies. We'll go this weekend!"

Sonia's eyes shone with anticipation. Lisa made herself a promise to introduce her little sister to all the joys that a teenager deserved. She vowed to make up for all the crucial years she had missed in her sister's life.

Mrs. Cohen came in as Lisa was packing her suitcase. "I haven't asked you lately how your music is going," said the matron, visibly saddened by Lisa's departure.

"All right, I guess," Lisa said, not sharing that she hadn't been able to practice.

"We're all looking forward to your concert," the matron said.

Lisa couldn't find the courage to tell her that she would have to cancel her debut, since try as she might, she couldn't find the strength to continue.

Mrs. Cohen stood by awkwardly as Lisa made her bed. Finally she spoke, breaking the reserve that she had kept for so long.

"I was thinking back to that afternoon when you first played our piano . . . when you thought you were sneaking in and no one would hear you."

Lisa kept smoothing her bed, finding it difficult to remember such an innocent time.

"I remember standing outside for fifteen minutes—afraid that if I came in, you might stop," Mrs. Cohen confessed, wiping away an uncharacteristic tear with her embroidered handkerchief.

"Perhaps I have waited too long to tell you this, but we, I . . . owe you so much. You have inspired us all."

Lisa turned around and accepted her warm embrace. Then the matron smiled sadly and backed out the door.

Sonia helped Lisa finish cleaning out her drawers, folding her dozens of scarves, and placing her costume jewelry in a velvet bag. Then, saving them for last, Lisa took her most prized possessions, the photos of her mother and father, and her grandmother's silver bag, and laid them reverently on top of her clothes, shutting the lid on the large suitcase and on a long chapter of her life.

Lisa left 243 Willesden Lane with her two suitcases and walked slowly down the road to Mrs. Canfield's. The woman in black embraced her warmly when she arrived on the doorstep. "This house has been quiet for too long. It has missed thee."

As she had done years before, Lisa unpacked her things in the son's room. His picture on the dresser now had a black ribbon tied around it.

One week after Lisa's departure, Mrs. Cohen received a call in the foyer of the hostel that brightened her spirits immensely. In the midst of the sea of disaster engulfing the community came a ripple of good news, a ripple that she knew would be a tidal wave for two of her "dear ones."

She hung up the phone, ran out the door, and went bustling down the block in her sensible shoes. She was out of breath when she made it to Riffel Road.

"Lisa, Lisa! You must call Mr. Hardesty at once!"

"What? What is it?" Lisa cried.

"You must call Mr. Hardesty at once," she repeated, picking up Mrs. Canfield's telephone and dialing for her.

Five long days later, an elegant Lisa and a well-scrubbed Sonia were picked up by Mr. Hardesty's waiting car and taken to Liverpool station to meet the 2:22 train.

Lisa and Sonia clung to each other and waited an eternity for the train to stop. When the doors opened, a group of weary refugees appeared, walking slowly down the stairs, their faces gaunt and haggard, exhausted by the trip and by misfortune. Lisa watched as they descended onto the platform and came toward her, disappearing and reappearing into the blast of steam that enveloped them. She strained to see into the approaching line of ragged people in heavy old world overcoats. She began to tremble, imagining she was seeing the ghostly apparitions of all her cherished neighbors from Franzenbrückestrasse.

The more Lisa strained to see, the more she trembled, and Sonia had to put her arms around her shoulders to hold her up.

After another eternity, they saw an outstretched hand waving in their direction and a familiar voice shouting from down the quay.

"Lisa! Lisa! Sonia! Sonia!"

Sonia pushed Lisa forward, and from inside the mass of the crowd came a thin, handsome woman, running as fast as she could. It was Rosie. It was Rosie at last. The three sisters flew into an embrace.

They called out one another's names, over and over, "Rosie, Sonia, Lisa!" reveling in each consonant and vowel, over and over again.

When Lisa could finally pry her eyes off her sister, she looked up at Leo, who was waiting patiently for his turn to embrace them. She grabbed him around the waist and almost tripped on a beautiful four-year-old girl who was looking up at her in wonder.

Lisa gasped.

"This is our little Esther," Rosie announced. "Isn't she beautiful?" Then turning to the little girl, said: "Esther, these are your aunties, Lisa and Sonia."

Lisa's eyes were so filled with tears she could barely see. Sonia knelt down and gave the little girl a kiss.

They went to the same restaurant in the station where Lisa had been taken with Sonia so long ago. The intervening years of war had removed the white tablecloths, and the elegant teapots had long ago been melted down for airplane parts. It was now a dingy cafeteria, but no one seemed to mind.

Leo was anxious to tell the sisters how he and Rosie had survived the last few years. Out spilled the story of their escape from Vienna as drunken tourists, the trip to freedom in Paris, then Paris fallen to Hitler, then running, and running some more.

"We were always running!" Rosie explained.

"Except when we were rounded up in a holding camp outside of Lyon," Leo interjected.

"Leo always found a way to escape," Rosie said proudly.

"It wasn't just me, there were many people who hid us."

"Until I had the baby."

Lisa and Sonia were looking with such love and admiration at their older sister that they were speechless.

"Then what happened?" Lisa begged.

"When Rosie was nine months pregnant, no one would take us in anymore, so she had to deliver the baby on the streets of Marseilles. Then we kept running until we made it to the Swiss border."

"Leo had to lift me over the barbed wire," Rosie broke in. "There were Nazis shooting at us from the French side. Just after he threw Esther to one of the Swiss guards, he got shot."

"Just in the leg," Leo said.

Sonia started to cry.

"We never gave up hope that we would see you again," Rosie whispered.

Then the tables were turned—Rosie and Leo begged to hear all about Lisa's and Sonia's lives since their separation. When Lisa told of her scholarship, Rosie took her daughter's hand and told her, "Your aunt Lisa is a wonderful pianist—just like your grandmother. . . ."

Finally, Lisa had to ask the question they had all been waiting to ask from the moment her sister stepped off the train.

"Rosie . . . do you have any news of Mama and Papa?"

Rosie looked at her sister with tears in her eyes.

"None of our letters were answered . . . I have heard nothing," she answered, then sadly pleading: "So then, you have heard nothing also?"

"Nothing," Lisa said. "We have heard nothing."

They could not bear to discuss it further, it was too hard. Rosie looked at her two younger sisters. "Mama would be so proud of you two," she said softly. "And Lisa, you know what your music meant to her . . . to all of us . . . look!"

Rosie leaned over and parted the buttons of Esther's coat. Around the little girl's neck was the chain that held the tiny gold charm of a piano.

"You have it?" Lisa cried, surprised.

Sonia spoke up. "I gave it to Rosie when I left on the train, just like you gave it to me. . . ."

Rosie put her arm around Sonia and said to Lisa, "And I never took it off, until I gave it to Esther."

Overwhelmed with the emotion of seeing the tiny charm around the neck of her new niece, Lisa felt the wall she had built up around her music beginning to give way. The forgotten promise she had made to her mother echoed in her heart.

She returned to her practicing with a fervor that surprised even Mrs. Floyd. She practiced every day from the moment she awoke until the Royal Academy closed its doors at night, throwing all her energy and passion into her preparation. For how would the next generation know of the music, the music Malka so loved, if she didn't honor her promise?

26

$\mathcal{L}$ISA SAT nervously at the mirror in the dressing room of the venerable Wigmore Hall, drumming her fingers on the countertop between the bottles of face paint, eyeliner, and rouge, and tried to sit still as her sister applied a bold brown stripe above her eyelashes.

"Ooh, perfect! You look just like Rita Hayworth!" said Rosie, putting on the last dab and returning the brush to the table. Rosie then checked her own makeup in the mirror and wiped a smudge from above her red lips. Life and color had returned to her older sister's face; she looked as sophisticated as Lisa remembered her.

But it was Lisa who was the knockout tonight. She shimmered in her red gown as she stood up and straightened the dark seams of her silk stockings and tried to calm her wildly beating heart.

Sonia ran into the dressing room from the stage, where she had been peeking out from the wings at the gathering crowd.

"It's almost full!" she cried excitedly.

"Don't go out there! They'll see you."

"No, they won't!"

"Yes, they will!" Lisa insisted.

"Relax, the two of you, you're making *me* nervous," said Rosie intervening.

The ornate turn-of-the-century hall, with its red velvet seats, was filling up quickly. Rosie had invited every person she met—people on the street, the butcher at the corner—every last soul in the beauty parlor. She knew instinctively it was important to have a packed concert hall for the full effect of this important night. And of course, the students and faculty of the Royal Academy would also be there.

She had also insisted that Lisa invite the nice French soldier whose address she had come across in Lisa's night table.

"He's probably in Paris, for heaven's sake," Lisa had said.

"You said you'd invite him, so you have to invite him! I'll pay for the telegram. You never know. People get around these days."

Lisa knew he would never come, she'd met him almost a year ago, but it didn't hurt to dream.

Mrs. Cohen had organized an early dinner for everyone at the hostel so they could get to the center of London at seven o'clock sharp. She didn't want anyone's stomach growling during the concert. She helped the youngest ones tie their ties and comb their hair, then clucked and scolded them out of the house at five-thirty, just in case the bus was late.

Lisa's mind raced as she adjusted the straps of her gown. She thought for a moment about how much had changed since her childhood fantasies of playing concerts for Viennese royalty. Instead of those adolescent dreams, she tried to focus on this audience, filled with the good people of England, the working people as well as the rich people, the friends as well as the strangers. There would be no dukes and counts, she chided herself.

But this was just a speech she gave herself to calm down. It wasn't working, however, and her heart started beating faster and faster. Her sisters wished her well one last time, and she was left alone. The hush was falling; the curtain was rising.

Lisa walked elegantly onto the stage and was greeted by enthusiastic applause, as she sat at the nine-foot Steinway grand. Its ebony finish was polished to perfection; its lid was fully open, reflecting the gleaming inner workings of the strings.

With a subtle adjustment of her posture, she brought a hush over the audience. Once all was silent, Lisa waited a few breaths until the air of expectation was almost unbearable, then took another deep breath and went inside herself. When she felt the audience disappear, she lifted her hands in a graceful arch and began.

Her first chords were somber but eloquent; she was starting, as she had at the audition, with Beethoven's *Pathétique*. This time, however, her opening was more confident and mature; she had the courage to start quietly, as her mother had often counseled. She began her story with the pianissimo that recalled the quiet despair of the agonizing separation from her family these past six years. The music deepened into thunderous chords retelling the years spent defiantly warding off the Nazi attacks. Lisa searched within herself and found the colors and shadings to express the depths of her longings and the heights of her triumphs.

As the intensity began to build, she sent her prayer across the footlights into the hearts of the people who had gathered together. The beauty of the music entered their souls, from the refugee to the barrister, from the garment worker to the RAF pilot, from the Resistance hero to the dockworker, and helped to guide them through their deepest, inexpressible emotions.

Mrs. Cohen's eyes were shining and devout as she allowed herself to remember and mourn her husband and sister, surely lost. Hans listened with a joy that surpassed that of any moment he had spent with Lisa in the cellar, the music bringing warmth to his darkness.

In the simple, dignified melody of the Chopin Nocturne in C-sharp Minor, Mrs. Canfield faced the loss of her son, John, reliving the images of his infancy and childhood and hearing in the music the heroism of his service as a medic. In Mrs. Canfield's mind, Lisa imbued the regal tones with her son's life story, one hand taking over from the other as she made the nostalgic notes evoke his life, lost but quietly remembered.

Gina and Gunter held tightly to one another and felt the excitement of their future in the nocturne's tender passages, their hearts rejoicing in the passion of Lisa's playing.

Mrs. McRae, Mr. Dimble, Mrs. Floyd, Mr. Hardesty, all of them in their way shared feelings they could never express in words. Lisa wove their stories through the Chopin and the Rachmaninoff, the music becoming the tale of so many in war-torn London.

She relived her own joys and tragedies, her terrible journey to London, and her passage to adulthood. She mourned her lost parents in the tragic tolling of the bells of the Rachmaninoff prelude; then, from its majestic progression of chords, she built a hymn of gratitude—to her parents' love, to their wise devotion, and to every mother and father who had the courage to save their child by saying good-bye.

When enough tears had been shed in the audience, Lisa began the final piece, Chopin's heroic polonaise. This was Lisa's tour de force, and its thunderous exuberance raised the spirits of all assembled as row after row of shining eyes relived their proudest, bravest moments—their courage under the bombing, their unshakable resolve, their ultimate victory.

There were many seconds of awed silence, then the audience erupted in tumultuous applause. Lisa stood up and the applause redoubled. She looked into the audience and took bow after bow before leaving the stage and the glory of the spotlight.

The scene in the dressing room was utterly chaotic. The press of people included all the hostel children, shaking Lisa's hand one by one, ten women from the factory, Mr. Hardesty and the staff of the Jewish Refugee Agency, Mrs. Canfield and five Quaker brethren, and, of course, Sonia and Rosie and Leo and Esther.

Then came Mabel Floyd, towing a well-dressed impresario, who congratulated her profusely and spoke loudly to be heard above the din: "Your professor tells me you play a wonderful Grieg piano concerto!"

Hans sat on a chair near Lisa and drank in the sound of the compliments, nodding his head in delight. Next to him stood Gina and Gunter. When Mrs. Cohen had finished escorting the younger children of the hostel through the informal receiving line, she asked them to stay back a minute while she said her own congratulations.

The matron watched the gracious young woman in the red gown thanking the well-wishers for their compliments and pulled out her embroidered handkerchief. The beautiful vision was too much for her.

"When did this happen? You are no longer children!" she exclaimed.

Lisa, Gina, and Gunter took her by the hand. "But we are," said Lisa. "We will always be the children of Willesden Lane."

At the stage door, behind another crush of well-wishers, stood a handsome French Resistance soldier wearing a discreet medal on the lapel of his uniform. He was waiting for the crowd to thin and was carrying a rare bottle of Mumm's champagne and a dozen red roses.

Rosie saw him first and, guessing who he must be, brought him over to her radiant sister. Lisa couldn't believe her eyes; she had tried to forget the image of this handsome soldier, it seemed so unlikely that they would ever meet again.

He put his hands over his heart, as he had before, to show how much he loved the music, then handed her the red roses with a card that read: "With fervent admiration, Michel Golabek."

Lisa clasped his hand and brought him into the group of well-wishers forming a tight circle around her. Through eyes brimming with tears, she surveyed the group that meant everything in the world to her, from Gina and Gunter to Hans and Mrs. Cohen, to her beautiful sisters, Sonia and Rosie, with Leo and Esther just behind, and now this handsome stranger who she instinctively felt would be part of her future.

Then, elated by the love and admiration surrounding her, she suddenly sensed an additional presence and was overwhelmed by a feeling of closeness to her mother. It was as if Malka were watching from above. Her heart filled with joy as she realized she had done it. She had fulfilled the promise she had made to her mother. She had held on to her music.

Lisa Jura, 1947.

Epilogue

*A*ARON WENT to America, married, and became a successful businessman. Gunter and Gina also immigrated to America, where they have lived together happily for more than fifty years. Hans remained in England, received his degree as a physical therapist, and went on to win numerous national chess championships for the blind. After closing the hostel at Willesden Lane, Mrs. Cohen lived with her son until her death at age seventy.

In the fall of 1949, Lisa Jura received a visa allowing her to immigrate to America. Michel Golabek was awarded the French Croix de Guerre in 1945 and followed Lisa to the United States shortly after she immigrated. They were married in New York in November 1949. They moved to Los Angeles, joining Rosie and Leo, who had settled there, and were followed by Sonia and her husband, Sol. The sisters remained in daily contact the rest of their lives.

In 1958, Lisa Jura was contacted by a long-lost cousin living in Israel, who wrote her the truth of what happened to Malka and Abraham. The cousin had received Abraham's last known communication, a letter written in January of 1942, which had been rerouted around the world to Palestine.

Abraham wrote of their pending deportation and implored the cousin with the words "We are lost . . . and beg you to look after our precious children."

On April 14, 1942, they were arrested by the Gestapo, taken from their home on Franzenbrückestrasse, and deported to Lodz. From there, they were sent to Auschwitz.

Lisa Jura had two daughters, Mona and Renée, who grew up to fulfill their mother's dream by becoming concert pianists.

Lisa's three granddaughters, Michele, Sarah, and Rachel, also play the piano. Her grandson, Yoni, plays the violin.

In June 1999, Lisa's daughters and granddaughters were invited to be the featured artists at the sixtieth worldwide reunion of the Kindertransport in London. Performing the "Clair de Lune" on the BBC, Michele and Sarah thanked Britain for saving Lisa's life and spoke of the precious words given to them by their grandmother and piano teacher. "Hold on to your music. It will be your best friend."

It continues to be.